INDIAN INS
COOK

The Healthy Indian Instant Pot Recipe Cookbook for Beginners

By

Alex Hansh

TABLE OF CONTENTS

Introduction

Thank you for purchasing this book *Indian Instant Pot Cookbook: The Healthy Indian Instant Pot Recipe Cookbook for Beginners*!

Today you will learn more about:

- Basic of Indian Culinary
- Benefits of Using Instant Pot
- Different parts and accessories of Instant Pot
- How to use Instant pot
- Indian Instant Pot Paneer Recipes
- Indian Instant Pot Fish and Meat Recipes
- Indian Instant Pot Vegan Recipes
- Indian Instant Pot Dals, Soups and Lentils Recipes
- Indian Instant Pot Salads Recipes

Since this is entirely made as a beginner's guide for new Instant Pot users, the book breaks down all the main parts, accessories of the Instant pot and their uses. Consider this book as a manual too as it explains the different ways to use the multicooker.

A quick preview of the Indian Cuisine will tell you more about their regular use of spices on most dishes. Recipes included in this book contains spices that Indians mostly uses on basic recipes. Each recipe has information on preparation time, cook time and serving size to help you better in cooking.

There are notes at the end of recipes to help you substitute some ingredients that might not be available in your pantry. For vegan, you may substitute oils with butter or healthy oils such as avocado oil, etc.

If you're ready, let's start cooking!

CHAPTER 1: Indian Food

Indian food culture is very different from American dishes not only in taste but also in the way these dishes are cooked. It's a blend of different culture and age. The overall development of foods in India has also been influenced by different civilizations.

When we think of Indian cuisine, we can't remove the word "spices". That is what their dishes are known for. Spices are used generously in their food, whether in Northern or Southern India. And every single spice they use has nutritional and medicinal properties.

However, cuisine differs across India's regions as a result of variation in local culture, geographical location and economics. It also varies seasonally, depending on which fruits and vegetables are ripe.

CHAPTER 2: Instant pot

The Instant Pot is a multi-cooker tool that does almost everything including a slow cooker, electric pressure cooker, rice cooker, steamer, yogurt maker, sauté/browning pan, and warming pot. It's made to cater to the needs of health-minded individuals, those with special dietary restrictions, the do-it-yourself food enthusiasts and basically anyone looking to save time in the kitchen. Just one cooker to do a lot of task.

Benefits of Using Instant Pot

Since an Instant pot is a multi-cooker, you get the work done in just one tool. Here are the benefits of using an Instant Pot:

12 single-key operation

Instant Pot has 12 single-key operation buttons for cooking:

- Rice
- Multigrain rice
- Congee/Porridge
- Sauté/Browning
- Soup
- Poultry
- Meat & Stew
- Beans & Chili
- Steaming
- Slow Cook
- Keep warm
- Yogurt

These one-button operation keys are designed to achieve good cooking results based on what you are cooking. What's even better is that each function button can further be refined to vary food taste in the range of "rare", "normal" and "well-done".

Automatic Cooking

In terms of convenience, the Instant Pot has fully automated cooking process, timing each cooking task and switch to keep-warm after cooking. There is no need to set you pressure keeping time when you are cooking, you can do so with the manual setting of the Instant pot.

Planning Meal with Delayed Cooking

This wonderful device has the capability to delay your cooking up to 24 hours, allowing you to plan the meal ahead of time. You don't have to be around the kitchen to manage the cooking. This device does the work on its own. You are no longer required to the kitchen to make the meal. Isn't it amazing that when you come home after work, you don't have to get dinner on the table in a hurry?

Traps Flavor, Vitamins and Minerals

The instant pot is sealed when cooking meals. This means that the nutrients and the aroma stay intact with the ingredients instead of diffusing around the house. The juice of fish, meat, and fruits remains within the food.

When using Instant pot to steam foods, there is no need for large amount of water. You just need enough water to keep the pressure cooker filled with steam so vitamins and minerals will not be dissolved by water.

Tender & Tasty Foods

Meat and bones can be cooked easily with Instant Pot. After cooking, the bones pork ribs are separated from the meat. They become chewable so the calcium and other minerals can be easily absorbed by our body. If you cook whole grain and beans recipes under pressure cooking, they become softer in texture and taste even better than normal cooking method.

10 Safety Features

This technology revolutionized the safety of pressure cooking. All safety parameters are discussed briefly below.

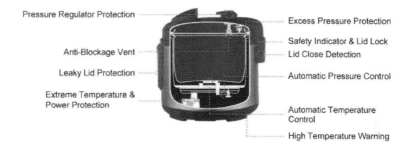

1. Lid Close Detection

Instant Pot will not activate pressurized cooking if the lid is missing or not closed properly. Only the keep-warm and sauté functions work with the lid being open.

2. Leaky Lid Protection

Just in case the steam release is not closed properly or the sealing ring is missing, the Instant pot will not reach preset pressure level. Instant Pot detects this by measuring the pre-heating time. If the pre-heating time is longer than expected, the Instant pot is designed to be switched to Keep-warm to avoid burning the food.

3. Lid Lock under Pressure

If the instant pot is pressure cooking, the lid will be locked to prevent accidental opening.

4. Anti-blockage Vent

The Instant Pot has specially structured vent shield to prevent jamming the steam release while cooking.

5. Automatic Temperature Control

The thermostat regulates the temperature of the inner pot to be within a safe range, based on the type of food being cooked.

6. High Temperature Warning

If a cooker is operating without water or moisture, there will be no pressure in the pot which will then lead to overheating. Overheating may also be caused by missing inner pot, inner pot not in proper contact with heating element, or inner pot having heat dissipation problem. No worries! The Instant Pot is designed to stop heating when the temperature went over a certain limit.

7. Extreme Temperature & Power Protection

Instant Pot is equipped with a special fuse which disconnects power at excessively high temperature and extremely high electrical current.

8. Automatic Pressure Control

The pressure sensor mechanism of the cooker keeps the pressure in a safe range when cooking.

9. Pressure Regulator Protection

If the pressure exceeds a certain limit, the steam release will be pushed up to allow the steam being released to bring down the pressure inside the pot.

10. Excess Pressure Protection

In case the pressure becomes too high and pressure regulator protection malfunctioned, Instant Pot's internal protection mechanism will activate. It will shift the inner pot downwards to create a gap between the lid and the inner pot so the steam will be released from the gap into the internal chamber, which will stop heating.

Different Instant Pot Models

The main difference between the two main Instant Pot models is their size.

IP-LUX50 = 5 quart capacity and 900W heating element

IP-DUO50 = 5 quart capacity and 900W heating element

IP-LUX60 = 6 quart capacity and 1000W heating element

IP-DUO60 = 6 quart capacity and 1000W heating element

IP-DUO80 = 8 quart capacity and 1200W heating element

The IP-LUX50 and IP-DUO50 have a 5 quart capacity. The IP-LUX60 and the IP-DUO60 are larger with a 6 quart capacity. The exterior size of the larger 6 quart capacity models is about 2 cm (3/4 inch) taller than the smaller 5 quart capacity models.

The DUO is simply the updated version of the LUX model. The main difference in functionality between the new and older models of the Instant Pot is that the DUO model has the yogurt making button and the LUX does not.

Parts and Accessories

Before you start, you have to read your Instant Pot's manual. Each one is different depending on your cooker's model, but there are a number of parts every model should have. Different models will vary, but will generally have these components.

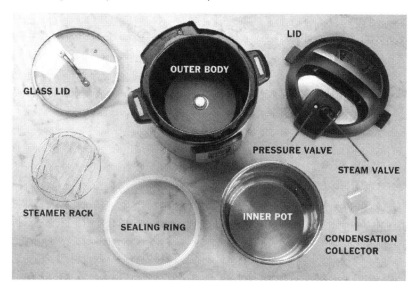

Outer Body: This is considered the brain of the machine. It has a display panel and various buttons for setting the functions. The outer body is what heats up when you turn on your Instant Pot. The inner pot goes inside the cooker's outer body. DO **NOT** cook food directly in the outer body if the inner pot isn't there.

Lid: The lid covers the pot. Make sure to lock the lid into place before the turning on the pressure cooking function. Some multicookers have detachable lids, and others have lids that are secured to the body of the pot on a hinge.

Pressure Valve: This metal valve specifies whether the cooker is pressurized or not. It will pop up when the cooker reaches pressure, and drop down when the pressure is released.

Some models have pressure valves hidden under plastic covers. If you own one, you may not be able to see the valve pop up or down.

Steam Valve: It allows the pot to build or release pressure. It has a sealing (locked) position and a venting (open) position. If you are cooking using the pressure cooking function, make sure that the valve is in the sealing position, or the pressure won't build. When using the slow cooking function, it must be in the venting position.

Condensation Collector: This plastic cup in the outer body of the pot catches any condensation released during slow cooking. This is not used when pressure cooking since the steam is contained in the pot.

Inner Pot: This is where the food cooks. It should be removed for cleaning every after use.

Sealing Ring: This surrounds the lid and helps seal steam into the pot. It can absorb the odor of strongly scented foods, like garlic, ginger and onions, during the cooking process. Always wash the sealing rings every after use.

Steamer Rack or Basket: This sits in the inner pot and keeps food raised above the liquid when you don't want it submerged.

How to use Instant pot

If this is your first encounter with an Instant pot, you might be confused. So many settings and buttons! You'll get to know them a bit later. Each button designates a type of cooking. Basically, buttons have preset cook times to make things easier for you. The setting on the buttons also indicate if the pot will be locked to capture steam when you pressure cook, or if you will be using the Instant Pot like a regular pot and cooking without pressure.

Water Test

This is one of the basic test to get to know how your pressure cooker comes to pressure by pressure cooking with just water.

1. Place insert into the Instant Pot.
2. Pour 2 cups of water into the insert.
3. Close the lid. It will chime when it's closed correctly.
4. Set the Pressure Release Valve to "sealing."
5. Press Manual.
6. Press the "-" button until 5 shows in the display. That's it. The Instant Pot does not have a start button. After about 30 seconds, the machine will turn on. The display will switch from "5" (shown above) to "On." The machine is now building pressure.
7. After about five minutes, the float valve should lift into place. You shouldn't see any steam leaking from the sides of the pot. Once the float valve seals the Instant Pot, the display will change from "On" to "5."
8. When the cook time completes, turn the pressure release valve to "venting." This is called a quick release Be sure to keep your hands and face away from the top of the pressure release valve. Hot steam pours out of it. (see video below)
9. Open the lid, away from your face, when the float valve drops.
10. That's it. You've completed the initial test of your Instant Pot!

Pressure Cooking

Of all the functions on an Instant Pot, pressure cooking is the one you'll probably use most often. It's much faster than a stove or an oven. It enables you to do shortcuts too, like making beans without soaking them first. It's also amazing to use pressure cooking in making tender and luscious meat.

How Does a Pressure Cooker Work?

With an electric pressure cooker, everything is done automatically. Once it reaches a certain pressure and temperature, it will stay there without you doing anything. You can set it and forget, much as you would with a slow cooker. It won't explode. It will simply turn itself off if the pressure or temperature ever rise too high.

Using Your Electric Pressure Cooker

Check your recipe, and set the device to the correct pressure level (high or low), then add the exact time you want your food to cook. High pressure is used for most recipes, with low used more often for quicker cooking and more delicate ingredients, like seafood, custards, some rice dishes and eggs.

After you set everything up, the clock won't immediately begin to count down. The pot must first build pressure before it starts counting down. Depending on the food you are cooking, this may take 5 to 20 minutes. When using this function, always make sure that the steam valve is in the locked or sealed position otherwise pressure cannot build if the device is in venting position.

How to Release Instant Pot When Pressure Cooking

You can release pressure in the Instant Pot in two ways. There is the *natural release method*, and the *quick release method.*

The natural release method allows the pressure to naturally disperse on its own while the quick release method is when you turn the valve on top of the pot from the "sealing" setting to the "venting" setting.

The Instant Pot naturally depressurizes by dispersing heat from the cover, specifically the metal parts. Depending on the volume of liquid in the cooking pot, it may take approximately 10-30 minutes to depressurize naturally. Basically, the more liquid content, the longer it takes. You can also place a towel soaked with cold water on the metal part of the lid to help cool the pot down.

On the other hand, the quick release method is used by manually turning the steam release handle to the "venting" position to let the steam out of the cooker. With quick release the Instant Pot takes 1-2 minutes to depressurize. The Instant Pot's steam release handle is a safety device that lets the steam seep quickly from the pot. It is not recommended to use the quick release method if you're cooking food with a high starch content to avoid food from spilling out of the steam release handle.

Make sure to wait until the Instant Pot has released all of the steam that has built up inside **before** you open it and take of the lid. DO **NOT** force the lid open. Keep your hand away from the top of the valve so you won't burn yourself when the hot steam vents. You may also turn the valve from a distance, with the help of a tongs or the handle of a wooden spoon. I'd recommend covering the valve with a dish towel before opening it to keep the steam from spraying all over your kitchen. If you are going to use your hands, be careful in approaching the valve from the side rather than the top.

Slow Cooking

This function allows you to cook your food very, very slowly, and it's perfect for when you want to do slow cooker recipes. You have the option to cook food at high or low, depending on your cooker's model. ON some models, you can cook slowly with a separate, clear glass cover so you can monitor your foods while on other models, you have to lock the lid on as if you were going to pressure cook the food.

Yogurt Making, Sautéing and Other Uses

The Instant pot can do more than just pressure cooking and slow cooking. Depending on your model, it also features several settings for preparing yogurt, rice or poultry, as well as sautéing.

Yogurt Setting

This function varies based on the recipe and your Instant Pot's model. Most yogurt functions will heat the pot at 180 degrees to 200 degrees to kill any bacteria in the milk while helping the yogurt to thicken. Then it keeps the milk at 110 degrees for several hours, during which time it ferments.

Saute Setting

This function works like a burner on your stove, heating the inner pot from the bottom up, and allowing you to brown meats and vegetables, and to simmer sauces to reduce them. It has several levels, from low to high, allowing you to adjust the heat. If yours doesn't, and the food is turning dark quickly, turn off the pot for a few minutes to bring down the heat. Then, if necessary, turn it back on. Or, you can always brown the ingredients on the stove in a skillet, then transfer them to the pot for the rest of the cooking. Make sure that when sautéing, the pot's lid should always be off.

Other Settings

You can experiment with any other functions if your Instant Pot model has them (rice, beans, poultry, steam). They always cook foods under pressure, and they're preprogrammed with the amount of time and pressure level needed for most function. It's going to be more precise to follow a recipe and manually set the exact time and amount of pressure. Then feel free to use the preset buttons as you get more comfortable.

CHAPTER 3: Indian Instant Pot Recipes

Paneer

Paneer Butter Masala

Prep Time: 10 minutes

Cook Time: 25 minutes

Serving: 2

INGREDIENTS:

- 1 lb Paneer chunks
- 1 tsp Cumin seeds
- 1 Onion (chopped)
- 4 Tomatoes (chopped)
- 1 Green chili
- 1 inch Ginger
- 8 cloves Garlic
- 2 tbsp Butter
- 1/4 cup Cashews
- 1/4 cup Cream
- 2 tbsp Dried Methi leaves

- 1 tbsp Honey
- 1 1/2 tsp Salt
- 1/4 cup Water

For small Spices:

- 1/2 tsp Turmeric
- 1 tsp Coriander
- 1 tsp Garam Masala
- 1/2 tsp Red Chili

For Big Spices:

- 2 sticks Cinnamon
- 5 Cardamom
- 2 Black Cardamom
- 1 tsp Black peppercorns
- 1 tsp Cloves

For garnish:

- dry fenugreek leaves

INSTRUCTIONS:

1. Put all the big spices into a cheesecloth to make a spice pouch. Tie it well so the spices will not come out of the pouch.
2. Except the paneer, put all the rest of the ingredients to the Instant Pot including the small spices.
3. Select manual mode on Instant pot and cook it for 15 minutes.
4. After 15 minutes, let the pressure release naturally.
5. Remove the spice pouch carefully.
6. Use an immersion blender to blend all the contents in the instant pot until it becomes a smooth paste.
7. Add the paneer into the instant pot. Bring to a boil.
8. Garnish with dry fenugreek leaves as desired.
9. Serve and enjoy!

Paneer Indian Soft Cheese

Prep Time: 10 minutes

Cook Time: 10 minutes

Serving: 6

INGREDIENTS:

- 1 quart half and half
- 1/4 cup white vinegar

INSTRUCTIONS:

1. Pour both ingredients into the Instant pot. Cook at low pressure for about 4 minutes.
2. Let the pressure release naturally for 10 minutes. Release the pressure.
3. The milk should separate into curds and a watery whey. Stir well.
4. Pour the mixture through cheesecloth.
5. Gather up the cheesecloth and put a heavy weight on it. This is to let the whey drain while the paneer forms a cohesive block.
6. Use a mold to form a nice square block.
7. Use a can of beans to weight it down and to help the whey drain.

Butter Tofu Paneer

Prep Time: 15 minutes

Cook Time: 30 minutes

Serving: 4

INGREDIENTS:

For Baking Tofu "Paneer"

- 12 oz firm cubed tofu
- ½ tsp garam masala
- ½ tsp paprika
- ½ tsp salt
- ½ tsp turmeric
- 2 tsp ginger (paste or minced)
- 2 tsp garlic (paste or minced)
- 2 tsp lemon juice
- 1.5 tsp water
- 1.5 tbsp cornstarch
- 1 tsp nutritional yeast (optional)
- 1 tsp oil

For making the Butter Sauce:

- 1 tsp oil or vegan butter
- 3 cloves garlic (chopped)
- 1 15 oz can diced tomatoes
- 1 inch cube of ginger
- 1 hot or mild green chile
- Cashews
- ½ to 1 cup water
- 1 tsp dried fenugreek leaves
- ½ tsp salt
- ½ tsp sugar

For spices:

- ½ tsp garam masala
- ½ tsp paprika
- ¼ to ½ tsp cayenne

INSTRUCTIONS:

Instructions for baked tofu:

1. Press the tofu in between paper towels for 10 minutes. Then cube them.
2. In a bowl, mix the rest of the ingredients under baked tofu, to make a marinade.
3. Make a marinade by mixing the rest of the ingredients for Baking Tofu "Paneer" in a bowl.
4. Add in the tofu and marinade for 15 minutes if possible.
5. Preheat the oven to 400 degrees F. Place the tofu cubes on parchment paper and bake for 20 minutes.

Instructions for the Butter Sauce:

1. Put the instant pot on sauté mode over medium heat. Add garlic and cook until golden.
2. Using a blender, puree the tomato with the chopped ginger and half the green chile.
3. Add the mixture to the instant pot and cook until the puree starts to thicken.
4. Don't wash the blender yet. Use it to blend the cashews and water until smooth. Blend the cashews for a minute, let it rest for a minute and then blend again for about a minute for a creamy result.
5. Reserve 1 tbsp of the cream for garnish later. Add the rest of the cashew cream to the instant pot.
6. Add spices, fenugreek leaves, salt and sugar and mix well.
7. Use ½ cup water to rinse out your blender and add it to the instant pot. Mix well and bring to a boil.
8. Fold in the baked tofu. Let it simmer for a minute.

9. Add in the julienned ginger and green chile.
10. Mix half of the ginger and chile. Set aside the other half as garnish.
11. Pour a little of the cashew cream and other garnishes as desired.

NOTE:

You can use ¾ tsp garlic powder in substitute of 2 tsp garlic (paste or minced) and other starch such as arrowroot in exchange of cornstarch. You can also add in 1 bay leaf and 1 cinnamon stick with the garlic for additional flavor. Remove these before serving. Taste and adjust salt, heat (add cayenne) and sweet. Add more water if needed for preferred consistency. Add more cashew cream for creamier. Serve over Easy Garlic Naan, rice or roti.

Palak Paneer

Prep Time: 15 minutes

Cook Time: 20 minutes

Serving: 4

INGREDIENTS:

- 5 cups spinach
- 2 small onions (chopped)
- ½ cup sweet corn
- 1 tbsp garlic (grated)
- 2 tsp ginger (grated)
- 2 green chilies
- 1 tsp garam masala
- ½ tsp sugar
- ½ tsp cumin seeds
- pinch of hing
- 2 tbsp oil
- 2.5 tbsp mayonnaise
- 4-5 cashews
- 2 tbsp milk
- 2 tbsp paneer (grated)

For tasting and garnishing:

- salt
- 1 tsp honey
- freshly squeezed lemon juice
- 1 cup or more cubed paneer

INSTRUCTIONS:

1. Set the instant pot to high pressure and bring 1 cup water to a boil.

2. Add in sugar and 2-3 drops of lemon juice.
3. Add in washed spinach 1 cup at a time. Use a spoon to press them down. Then add another cup of spinach. Repeat the process until you have successfully added all the spinach to the pot.
4. Select manual mode on Instant pot and cook it for 5 minutes or until the spinach has wilted.
5. Strain spinach carefully and save the spinach stock later.
6. Transfer spinach to a bowl full of ice and some water.
7. Clean the Instant pot. Put the instant pot on sauté mode. Wait till it is hot and add oil, cumin and hing.
8. Add in onion puree, ginger garlic and stir well.
9. Set the instant pot to medium heat. Stir occasionally for 1- 2 minutes.
10. Add garam masala.
11. Use a blender to puree spinach, chilies, nuts, grated paneer and milk together.
12. Add the puree to the instant pot. Cook for 30 seconds.
13. Add in mayonnaise and honey. Stir well until smooth.
14. You can add spinach stock if the gravy is too thick
15. Cook for a minute more. Add salt to taste.
16. Add in the paneer and sweet corn. Cook for a minute.
17. Let the pressure release naturally for a few minutes.
18. Add in lemon juice as desired.
19. Serve and enjoy!

Vegetable and Paneer Biryani

Prep Time: 30 minutes

Cook Time: 20 minutes

Serving: 6

INGREDIENTS:

- 3 tbsp ghee divided
- 1 large onion thinly sliced
- 1 tsp cumin seeds
- 4 whole green cardamom
- 4 cloves
- 8-10 whole black pepper
- 2 bay leaves
- 3 tsp salt divided
- 1/2 cup fresh mint chopped
- 2 cups long-grain basmati rice
- 1/2 cup cilantro chopped

Veggies:

- 1 cup carrots chopped
- 1 cup green beans chopped
- 1 cup white mushrooms halved
- 1/2 cup red pepper chopped
- 1/2 cup corn
- 1 cup paneer cubed

Spices:

- 1/2 tbsp Ginger
- 1/2 tbsp garlic
- 1/4 tsp turmeric
- 1 tsp red chili powder
- 1 tsp garam masala

INSTRUCTIONS:

1. Rinse and soak the rice in 2 cups of water for 20 minutes. Drain and set aside for later.
2. Put the instant pot on sauté mode. Wait till it is hot and heat in oil.
3. add 1 tablespoon ghee and sliced onions. Cook for 5-7 mins until the onions are lightly caramelized.
4. Take half of the onions out and set aside for garnish later.
5. Add remaining ghee, cumin seeds, cardamom, cloves, black pepper, bay leaves. Cook for 30 seconds.
6. Add in the veggies, the spices and 1 tsp of salt. Mix well.
7. Add mint, rice and 2 tsp salt. Add 2 cups of water. Mix well. Make sure most of the rice is under water.
8. Close the lid and set the steam release handle to 'Sealing'.
9. Select manual mode on Instant pot and cook on high pressure for 6 minutes.
10. When cooking is complete, press Cancel and use quick release method by turning the valve on the lid from sealing to venting.
11. Open the lid. Garnish with caramelized onions and cilantro.
12. Serve and enjoy!

Saag Paneer

Prep Time: 10 minutes

Cook Time: 15 minutes

Serving: 4

INGREDIENTS:

- 1 tbsp Ghee or Oil
- 1/4 tsp Cumin seeds or Jeera
- 2 Green chili chopped
- 1 inch Ginger chopped
- 10 cloves Garlic chopped
- 2 Onion medium sized, sliced
- 9 oz Mustard leaves
- 9 oz Spinach or Palak chopped
- 10 oz Paneer or Cottage cheese cut into small pieces
- 2 tbsp Corn meal

Spices:

- 1/2 tsp Turmeric or Haldi powder
- 1/2 tsp Cayenne or Red Chili powder
- 2 tsp Coriander or Dhaniya powder
- 1 tsp Salt

INSTRUCTIONS:

1. Put the instant pot on sauté mode. Wait till it is hot and heat in the ghee.
2. Add jeera, green chili, ginger and garlic. Cook until the ginger and garlic turn golden brown.
3. Add the chopped onions. Sauté for 3 minutes.
4. Add the spices to the instant pot. Then add the mustard greens and spinach. Mix well.

5. Close the lid and set the steam release handle to 'Sealing'.
6. Select manual mode on Instant pot and cook on high pressure for 2 minutes.
7. When the instant pot beeps, let the pressure release naturally for 5 minutes.
8. Turn off the instant pot. Open the lid.
9. Add in the corn flour.
10. Use an immersion blender to blend the saag to a smooth paste.
11. Turn on the instant pot in sauté mode. Add in the paneer and cook for about 3 minutes.
12. Serve and enjoy!

NOTES:

If you don't have mustard leaves, you can just make it with spinach. Just double the quantity of spinach and keep the other ingredients the same.

Mutter Paneer Masala

Prep Time: 20 minutes

Cook Time: 10 minutes

Serving: 4

INGREDIENTS:

- 10 oz Paneer or Cottage cheese cubed
- 1 cup Green peas
- 1 Onion
- 2 Tomato
- 1 inch Ginger
- 4 cloves Garlic
- 1 Green chili
- 1 tbsp Oil
- 1 tsp Cumin seeds or Jeera
- 2 tbsp Cream or Malai
- 1 tbsp Coconut Cream or Coconut milk 1/4 cup (optional)
- 2 tbsp Kasuri Methi or Dried Methi leaves (Optional)
- 1 cup Water
- 2 tsp Salt
- Cilantro to garnish

Spices:

- 1/4 tsp Turmeric or Haldi powder
- 1/2 tsp Cayenne or Red Chili powder
- 1 tsp Coriander or Dhaniya powder

INSTRUCTIONS:

1. Grind onion, ginger, garlic and green chilli to make a paste.
2. Start the Instant Pot in sauté mode. Add oil and cumin seeds.

3. Once the cumin seeds start to splutter, add grinded paste. Cook for 4 minutes until the onions turn light brown. Grind tomatoes at the same time.
4. Once the onion is cooked, add the tomatoes paste to the instant pot and cook for another 4 minutes.
5. Stir in the spices and salt.
6. Roll the kasuri methi with your hand to make it a fine powder. Stir it in the instant pot.
7. Add the cubed paneer, green peas and water to the instant pot. Deglaze anything is stuck to the bottom of the pot.
8. Close the lid and set the steam release handle to 'Sealing'.
9. Select manual mode on Instant pot and cook on high pressure for 2 minutes.
10. When cooking is complete, press Cancel and use quick release method by turning the valve on the lid from sealing to venting.
11. Stir in the cream/malai and coconut cream.
12. Adjust the salt and spices as per your preference.
13. Garnish with cilantro. Serve and enjoy!

Paneer Tikka Masala

Prep Time: 5 minutes

Cook Time: 30 minutes

Serving: 4

INGREDIENTS:

- 10 oz Paneer, cubed
- 2 tablespoons unsalted butter
- 4-5 medium tomatoes, pureed
- 1/2 medium onion, chopped
- 1 tablespoon ginger-garlic paste (1/2 inch ginger + 3 cloves garlic, crushed)
- 1/2 cup heavy cream
- 2 teaspoon Garam Masala
- 2 teaspoon Coriander Powder
- 1 teaspoon Cumin Powder
- 1 teaspoon Turmeric Powder
- 1/2 teaspoon Paprika
- 1/2 teaspoon Red Chili Powder
- 1/2 teaspoon Cardamom Powder (optional)
- 2 teaspoon Kasoori Methi (dried fenugreek leaves)
- 1 teaspoon salt
- 1/4 cup water
- 1 tablespoons chopped cilantro for garnish

INSTRUCTIONS:

1. Chop onions, crush ginger-garlic, puree tomatoes, cube paneer as per ingredients instructions.
2. Put the instant pot on sauté mode. Wait till it is hot and add butter.

3. Add onions and sauté for 1 minute. Add ginger-garlic paste, sauté for 30 seconds.
4. Add tomato puree, 1/4 cup water and all spices. Stir well.
5. Add kasoori methi and half of the heavy cream, 1/4 cup. Save the remaining 1/4 cup for later. Stir well.
6. Close the lid and set the steam release handle to 'Sealing'.
7. Select manual mode on Instant pot and cook on high pressure for 3 minutes.
8. When the instant pot beeps, let the pressure release naturally for 5 minutes.
9. Open lid. Using an immersion blender, blend the curry into a smooth texture.
10. Set it back to sauté mode. Add paneer cubes, the remaining heavy cream. Simmer for 1-2 minutes.
11. Garnish with fresh cilantro as desired.
12. Serve with Naan or Jeera rice. Enjoy!

Fish, chicken meat

Chicken Tikka Masala

Prep Time: 10 minutes

Cook Time: 20 minutes

Serving: 4

INGREDIENTS:

- 2 tbsp olive oil
- 1 chopped onion
- 3 minced cloves garlic
- 1 1-inch piece of peeled and chopped ginger
- 2 tsp paprika
- 1 tsp garam masala
- 1 tsp ground turmeric
- 2 tsp cumin
- 1 tsp ground coriander
- ¼ tsp cayenne pepper
- 1 14 oz can diced tomatoes (with juice)
- 1.5 lbs boneless, skinless chicken breast
- ½ cup chicken broth
- ½ cup canned coconut milk
- Juice of 1 lemon
- 1 tbsp arrowroot starch
- Chopped fresh basil or cilantro

INSTRUCTIONS:

1. Set your instant pot to Sauté mode and turn to high heat. Wait till Instant pot is hot.
2. Add olive oil, ginger, onion, and garlic. Stir for 3-4 minutes.

3. Select cancel on your instant pot.
4. Add paprika, garam masala, ground turmeric, cumin, ground coriander and cayenne pepper to the mixture. Scrape from the bottom to form a paste.
5. Add the tomatoes and then stir.
6. Place the chicken on top then pour chicken broth on top.
7. Close the lid. Select manual on your Instant Pot and cook the dish on high pressure for about 6-8 minutes until it cooks.
8. Once cooked, use a quick release.
9. Remove the chicken from the Instant Pot and chop it using a fork since the chicken is tender.
10. Place chicken back into the Instant Pot.
11. Select sauté from the Instant Pot, and simmer for 4-5 minutes.
12. Add coconut milk.
13. If mixture is too thin, add arrowroot starch to the lemon juice, then pour into mixture.
14. Put salt into the mixture.
15. Once mixture is thick enough, serve with fresh basil or cilantro. Enjoy!

Double Up Indian Chicken Tikka Masala

Prep Time: 20 minutes

Cook Time: 20 minutes

Serving: 6

INGREDIENTS:

For marinating the chicken:

- 1 ½ pounds boneless, skinless chicken (breast or thighs), cut into large pieces
- ½ cups Greek yogurt
- 4 cloves garlic minced
- 2 tsp minced ginger minced
- ½ tsp turmeric
- ¼ tsp cayenne pepper
- ½ tsp smoked paprika for color and a slightly smoky taste
- 1 tsp salt
- 1 tsp garam masala
- 1/2 tsp ground cumin

For the sauce:

- 1 onion, chopped
- 1 14- oz can diced tomatoes
- 1 carrot, chopped
- 5 cloves garlic, minced
- 2 tsp minced ginger minced
- 1 tsp turmeric
- ½ tsp cayenne pepper
- 1 tsp paprika
- 1-2 tsp salt
- 2 tsp garam masala

- 1 tsp ground cumin

For finale:

- 4 oz half and half
- 1 tsp garam masala
- ¼-1/2 cup chopped cilantro

INSTRUCTIONS:

1. Marinate the chicken with the ingredients specified above.
2. Beat and blend the yogurt well so it doesn't separate later.
3. Set aside for 1-2 hours (if possible only).
4. Put the sauce ingredients into the Instant Pot.
5. Place the marinated chicken with the yogurt on top of the sauce ingredients.
6. Cook at High Pressure for 10 minutes and release pressure quickly.
7. Remove chicken and set aside.
8. Purée the sauce well using an immersion blender.
9. Add 1/2 cup of half and half and stir well.
10. Remove half the sauce and freeze for later.
11. Put chicken back into the remaining sauce
12. Mix in the garam masala.
13. Garnish with cilantro
14. Serve and enjoy!

Chicken Curry Recipe with Potatoes

Prep Time: 10 minutes

Cook Time: 15 minutes

Serving: 6

INGREDIENTS:

- 2 tsp olive oil
- 1/2 yellow onion (chopped)
- 1/2 Gala apple (chopped)
- 2 tbsp minced ginger
- 4 garlic minced cloves
- 6 tbsp mild curry paste
- 2 tsp ground coriander
- 2 tsp ground cumin
- 2 tsp garam masala
- 2 lb. boneless, skinless chicken thighs
- 1 lb. potatoes
- 1 1/2 cup diced tomatoes
- 3/4 cup chicken broth
- 3/4 cuplite coconut milk
- 1/2 tsp salt
- 1/2 tsp ground pepper

INSTRUCTIONS:

1. Put the instant pot on sauté mode. Add the olive oil and allow to heat for 1 minute.
2. Add the onion, apple and ginger. Cook for 5 minutes or until softened.
3. Stir in the garlic, curry paste, coriander, cumin and garam masala. Cook them for 1 minute.

4. Add the chicken thighs, potatoes, tomatoes, chicken broth, coconut milk, salt and pepper. Stir to combine.
5. Close the lid. Make sure the valve is sealed. Select manual mode on Instant pot and set to HIGH pressure for 10 minutes.
6. After 10 minutes, wait for 5 more minutes then let the pressure release naturally.
7. Shred the chicken with two forks.
8. Serve and enjoy!

NOTE:

Larger Creamer potatoes should be quartered and the smaller ones should be halved.

Chicken Curry Low Carb with Spinach & Yogurt

Prep Time: 10 minutes

Cook Time: 15 minutes

Serving: 6

INGREDIENTS:

For Sauce:

- 1 onion peeled & quartered
- 1 tablespoon garlic minced
- 1 tablespoon minced ginger minced
- 2 tomatoes quartered
- ½ cup greek yogurt
- 2 tablespoons corn starch
- 1 teaspoon salt
- ½ teaspoon cayenne pepper
- 2 teaspoon turmeric
- 1 teaspoon garam masala
- 1/2 c water

Other Ingredients:

- 1.5 pounds of chicken thighs, boneless, skinless
- 10 oz baby spinach
- 1 teaspoon garam masala

INSTRUCTIONS:

1. Using a blender, put all the ingredients for sauce and blend them together.
2. Place the large pieces of chicken in the Instant Pot.
3. Pour over the blended sauce on top of the chicken.
4. Put the instant pot on SOUP mode for 8 minutes.
5. Close the lid. Make sure the valve is sealed.

6. Let the pressure release naturally for about 10 minutes.
7. Open the lid. and remove the chicken.
8. Put the instant pot on sauté mode on MEDIUM.
9. Chop the spinach and add it to the sauce.
10. Chop the chicken into smaller chunks and add back into the pot.
11. Let the sauce to simmer and thicken with the lid off, and the spinach to cook down.
12. Add 1 teaspoon garam masala to add fragrance and flavor to the mixture.
13. Serve and enjoy!

NOTE:

If using other pieces of chicken aside from chicken thighs, adjust times per cooking charts.

You can use a food processor instead of a blender.

Serve with rice, cauliflower rice, naan, or with mashed potatoes.

Indian Butter Chicken

Prep Time: 10 minutes

Cook Time: 30 minutes

Serving: 5

INGREDIENTS:

- 2lbs boneless skinless chicken thighs
- 2 tbsp lemon juice
- 1 tsp Redmon Real Salt
- 3 tbsp Tin Star Foods Ghee
- 1 large sweet onion
- 2 inch piece of fresh ginger
- 3 garlic cloves
- 2 bay leaves
- 1 cinnamon stick
- 1 cup coconut milk
- 1 tsp apple cider vinegar
- 1 tbsp beef gelatin (optional, if using cashew milk/broth don't use it)
- 1/2 cup chopped almonds
- 1/2 bunch fresh cilantro

Spices:

- 1 tbsp garam masala
- 1 1/2 tbsp turmeric
- 1 tbsp cumin
- 1 tsp black pepper

INSTRUCTIONS:

1. Peel and slice your onion. Mince the garlic. Peel and slice the ginger.

2. Heat the instant pot on sauté mode. Add in the ghee.
3. Add in the onion, garlic, ginger and bay leaves. Saute for 5 minutes or until tender and aromatic.
4. Add in the chicken, all the spices and salt. Stir well.
5. Add in the lemon juice, apple cider vinegar and cinnamon stick. Stir well until the chicken is lightly browned.
6. Add in the coconut milk, stir and bring to a simmer.
7. Cancel the saute function. Stir in the gelatin.
8. Close the lid and set to pressure cook: poultry mode (about 20 minutes).
9. When it's done, release the pressure manually.
10. Open the lid and cancel the pressure cooker mode, set to reduce or saute mode.
11. Stir in the chopped almonds and simmer for about 10 minutes.
12. Garnish with cilantro as desired. Serve and enjoy!

Chicken Tikka Bites

Prep Time: 2 hours 3 minutes

Cook Time: 4 minutes

Serving: 1

INGREDIENTS:

- 1 Chicken Breast
- 3 Tbsp Greek Yoghurt
- ½ Lemon juice and rind
- Salt & Pepper

Spices:

- 1 Tsp Ginger Puree
- 1 Tsp Garlic Puree
- 1 Tsp Chilli Powder
- 1 Tsp Coriander
- 1 Tsp Cumin
- 1 Tsp Mixed Spice
- 1 Tsp Turmeric
- 1 Tsp Garam Masala
- 1 Tsp Masala Powder

INSTRUCTIONS:

1. Place a large strip of silver foil onto your worktop. Add all your spices to it.
2. Place the chicken breast on top and season it with salt and pepper.
3. Drizzle with your lemon juice and add your Greek yoghurt.
4. Seal it. Using a rolling pin, bash the side that has the spices to spread the flavor.
5. Place it in the fridge for at least 2 hours to marinate.

6. Place 200ml of water into the bottom of your Instant Pot add your steaming shelf and place the silver foil packet on top of that.

7. Turn the valve to sealing and cook your chicken tikka on the steam function for 4 minutes. When it beeps allow it to remain on the keep warm for a couple of minutes before serving it.

8. Slice it up into chunks and serve on skewers with salad as desired. Enjoy!

Apricot Chicken

Prep Time: 20 minutes

Cook Time: 11 minutes

Serving: 6

INGREDIENTS:

- 2 1/2 lbs chicken thighs bone-in skinless
- 1/2 tsp salt
- 1/4 tsp black pepper
- 1 tbsp vegetable oil
- 1 large onion chopped
- 1/2 cup chicken broth divided
- 1 tbsp Ginger grated fresh
- 2 cloves garlic minced
- 1/2 tsp ground cinnamon
- 1/8 tsp ground allspice
- 1 can diced tomatoes 14-oz can
- 1 package dried apricots 8-oz can

Optional:

- 1 pinch saffron threads
- Italian parsley chopped fresh

INSTRUCTIONS:

1. Season both sides of chicken with 1/2 teaspoon salt and 1/4 teaspoon pepper.
2. Put the instant pot on sauté mode. Wait till it is hot and add in oil. Add chicken in batches and cook for about 8 minutes or until browned on both sides. Remove to plate.

3. Add onion and 2 tablespoons broth to pot. Cook and stir for 5 minutes or until onion is translucent. Scrape up browned bits from bottom of pot.
4. Add in ginger, garlic, cinnamon and allspice. Cook and stir 30 seconds or until fragrant.
5. Stir in tomatoes, apricots, remaining broth and saffron, if desired. Mix well. Return chicken to pot, pressing into liquid.
6. Close the lid and set the steam release handle to 'Sealing'. Press Manual and cook at high pressure for 11 minutes.
7. When the pressure cooker beeps, press Cancel and do a quick pressure release. Season with additional salt and pepper.
8. Garnish with parsley as desired. Serve and enjoy!

Chicken Saag

Prep Time: 5 minutes

Cook Time: 15 minutes

Serving: 4

INGREDIENTS:

- 10 oz Spinach
- 1 lb Chicken thighs or chicken breasts, cut into 2-3 pieces
- 1 tablespoon Oil
- 1/2 teaspoon Cumin Seeds or Jeera
- 1 inch Ginger chopped
- 6 cloves Garlic
- 2 Onions medium sized, cut into pieces

Spices:

- 1/4 teaspoon Turmeric or Haldi powder
- 1/2 teaspoon Cayenne or Red chili powder
- 2 teaspoon Coriander or Dhaniya powder
- 1 teaspoon Salt

INSTRUCTIONS:

1. Put the instant pot on sauté mode. Wait till it is hot and heat in oil.
2. Add cumin seeds, ginger, and garlic. Stir well for about 30 seconds or until garlic turns golden. Add the cut onions. Saute for couple of minutes.
3. Add the spices and stir well.
4. Add the spinach and place the chicken pieces on top of the spinach. Press CANCEL and close the pressure cooker lid with vent in sealing position.

5. Press MANUAL or Pressure Cook mode for 8 minutes. When the pressure cooker beeps, press Cancel and do a quick pressure release.
6. Open the lid, remove the chicken pieces and set aside for later.
7. Using an immersion blender, blend the spinach and other ingredients to a creamy texture.
8. If needed, cut the chicken into smaller pieces and then add it back to the spinach curry.
9. Press SAUTE and give the curry a quick boil. This could splutter out, so cover with a lid. If the chicken is not well cooked, then boil for a bit longer.
10. Serve and enjoy with naan, roti or rice.

NOTES:

If you don't have an immersion blender, you could transfer the ingredients to a regular blender, blend to a smooth paste and then transfer them back in the instant pot insert.

Chicken Chettinad

Prep Time: 10 minutes

Cook Time: 20 minutes

Serving: 4

INGREDIENTS:

- 1 lb Chicken thighs boneless
- 1 tbsp Ghee or Oil
- 1 Bay leaf or Tej Patta
- 5 Curry leaves or Kadipatta
- 1" inch Ginger
- 5 cloves Garlic
- 1/4 cup Grated Coconut fresh or dry
- 1 Onion large, diced
- 2 Tomato medium, diced
- 1 tsp Salt adjust to taste
- 1/2 cup Water for cooking
- Cilantro to garnish

Whole Spices:

- 4 Red Chili Whole Kashmiri or another variety
- 1 tsp Black Peppercorns
- 1 tsp Cumin seeds or Jeera
- 2 tsp Coriander Seeds
- 5 Green Cardamom or Elaichi
- 1 stick Cinnamon or Dalchini
- 4 Clove or Laung
- 1 tbsp Poppy Seeds
- 1 tsp Fennel Seeds

INSTRUCTIONS:

Preparing Chettinad Spice blend:

1. Heat the Instant Pot in SAUTE mode. Add in all the whole spices and roast them for about 30 seconds or until aromatic. Add in ginger, garlic and grated coconut. Saute for another 30 seconds.
2. Press CANCEL to turn off the pressure cooker. Transfer all the ingredients in the pressure cooker to a blender. Grind to a powder or if needed add some water to make a paste.

Preparing Chettinad Chicken Curry:

1. Start the pressure cooker in SAUTE mode and heat oil in it. Add the bay leaf and curry leaves. Saute for 30 seconds.
2. Add the diced onion and saute for about 3 minutes.
3. Then add the diced tomatoes, ground spices and salt. Saute for 2 mins.
4. Add chicken pieces and saute for 3 minutes to infuse the spices in the chicken.
5. Add water for cooking. Press CANCEL and close the lid and set the steam release handle to 'Sealing'.
6. Change the setting to MANUAL or pressure cook mode on high pressure for 5 minutes.
7. When the pressure cooker beeps, press Cancel and do a quick pressure release.
8. Garnish with cilantro as desired. Serve and enjoy!

NOTES:

Cut the chicken pieces small, about 1-1.5 inch. If using larger pieces, increase the pressure cooking time by 2-3 minutes. You can substitute chicken breast for chicken thighs. If using bone-in chicken, increase the cooking time to 10 minutes.

Lamb Curry

Prep Time: 30 minutes

Cook Time: 20 minutes

Serving: 6

INGREDIENTS:

- 1 ½ lbs. cubed lamb meat
- 4 cloves garlic, minced
- 1-inch piece fresh ginger (grated)
- ½ cup coconut milk
- Juice of ½ lime
- ¼ tsp. sea salt + to taste
- Pinch of black pepper
- 1 tbsp. ghee
- 1 (14 oz.) can diced tomatoes
- 1 ½ Tbsp. garam masala
- ¾ tsp. turmeric
- 1 medium onion (diced)
- 3 medium carrots (sliced)
- 1 medium zucchini (diced)

For finale:

- Chopped cilantro

INSTRUCTIONS:

1. Combine lamb meat, minced garlic, grated ginger, coconut milk, lime juice, sea salt and black pepper in a container with a lid. Mix them and marinate in refrigerator for 30 minutes (up to 8 hours if possible).
2. Add meat with marinade, tomatoes with their juice, ghee, garam masala, onions and carrots.

3. Close the lid and set the steam release handle to 'Sealing'.
4. Select Manual mode and cook at high pressure for 20 minutes.
5. Then, let the pressure release naturally for 15 minutes.
6. Flip the steam release handle to 'Venting' to release the remaining steam before attempting to open the lid.
7. Remove the lid then switch the Instant Pot to sauté mode.
8. Stir in diced zucchini. Let it simmer for 5-6 minutes (without the lid) until zucchini is tender. Make sure sauce is slightly thickened.
9. Garnish with chopped cilantro and serve. Enjoy!

NOTE:

You may substitute chicken or beef for lamb meat. You may also substitute yellow curry powder for garam masala. Then, omit turmeric if you are going to use curry powder. Serve over rice or cauliflower rice.

Goan Pork Vindaloo

Prep Time: 25 minutes

Cook Time: 32 minutes

Serving: 6

INGREDIENTS:

- 2 lbs boneless pork loin chops
- 2 large potatoes (peeled and diced)
- 1 box chicken broth, 32 oz
- 1 large onion (diced)
- 4 cloves garlic (chopped)
- 1 one-inch piece ginger (chopped)
- 1 tsp turmeric
- 1-2 tsp tamarind concentrate
- ¼ cup cider vinegar
- salt and pepper

For Spices:

- 4-6 red chilis
- 1 bay leaf
- 1½ tsp cumin seeds
- 1½ tsp coriander seeds
- 1 two inch piece cinnamon stick
- 6 cloves
- 10 peppercorns
- 1 tsp mustard seeds

INSTRUCTIONS:

For the Spices:

1. Use a small pan and heat it on medium low.

2. Add the spices ingredients and roast them until fragrant.
3. Let it cool and grind.
4. Put the instant pot on sauté mode. Wait till it is hot and add the coconut oil.
5. Add in onions, ginger, and garlic. Sauté until onions turns golden.
6. Add the ground spices you made earlier and the turmeric. Stir well.
7. Add the pork, chicken broth, tamarind, and vinegar. Stir well.
8. Turn the instant pot off, then back on.
9. Close the lid, and switch the steam release switch to closed.
10. Press the button for meat/stew and adjust the time down to 25 minutes.
11. Once it's done, release the steam. Open the lid and taste.
12. Add salt and pepper to taste.
13. Add the potatoes. Close the lid back and close the steam switch.
14. Select manual mode on Instant pot and cook it for 7 minutes.
15. After 7 minutes, let the pressure release naturally.
16. Serve and enjoy!

54

Goat Curry

Prep Time: 10 minutes

Cook Time: 25 minutes

Serving: 4

INGREDIENTS:

- 1 lb Mutton bone-in
- 3 tbsp Ghee or Oil
- 1 Green Chili
- 1 large onion (chopped)
- 1/2 tbsp Ginger (minced)
- 1/2 tbsp Garlic (minced)
- 1 Tomato medium (chopped)
- 1 tbsp Lemon juice
- Cilantro

For Big Spices:

- 1/2 tsp Cumin seeds
- 6 Black peppercorns
- 6 Cloves
- 1 stick Cinnamon
- 1 Bay leaf
- 2 Black Cardamom

For small Spices:

- 1/4 tsp Turmeric
- 1 tsp Cayenne
- 2 tsp Coriander
- 1 tsp Garam Masala
- 1 tsp Salt

INSTRUCTIONS:

1. Put the instant pot on sauté mode. Wait till it is hot and add in oil to it.
2. Add all the ingredients for big spices. Sauté for 30 seconds and let them release the aroma.
3. Add the chopped green chili, onions, ginger and garlic to the pot. Cook for 4 minutes until they turn golden. Stir occasionally.
4. Add the chopped tomatoes and small spices. Mix and cook for 2 minutes.
5. Add the mutton into the pot. Mix well. Cook for 2 minutes.
6. Stir and scrape off anything stuck to the bottom of the pot.
7. Press Cancel and close the lid. Change the instant pot setting to MEAT mode for 20 minutes.
8. After 20 minutes, let the pressure release naturally.
9. Stir in the lemon juice.
10. Garnish with cilantro as desired.
11. Serve and enjoy!

Kheema Pav – Ground Chicken Curry

Prep Time: 5 minutes

Cook Time: 20 minutes

Serving: 4

INGREDIENTS:

- 1 tbsp oil
- 1 tsp cumin seeds
- 1/2 tsp turmeric
- 1 tbsp garlic grated
- 1 tbsp Ginger grated
- 1 large yellow onion diced
- 2 plum tomatoes diced
- 1 lb ground chicken
- 1/2 cup cilantro chopped for garnish

Spices:

- 2 tsp mild red chili powder
- 1 tsp garam masala
- 1 tsp salt
- 2 tbsp coriander powder

To serve:

- 1 tbsp butter or ghee
- 8 potato rolls

INSTRUCTIONS:

1. Put the instant pot on sauté mode. Wait till it is hot and heat in oil.
2. Add cumin seeds and toast for 30 seconds.
3. Add turmeric powder and mix well.

4. Add ginger and garlic. Mix well.
5. Add onion and sauté for a minute. Put the lid back on while cooking for 2 minutes.
6. Add in tomatoes and spices. Mix well.
7. Add ground chicken and break it with a spatula.
8. Add 1/2 cup of water. You can add 2 tablespoons of water for a thicker curry.
9. Close the lid and set the steam release handle to 'Sealing'.
10. Select manual mode on Instant pot and cook on high pressure for 4 minutes.
11. When the instant pot beeps, let the pressure release naturally for a few minutes.
12. Taste and adjust spice. Garnish with cilantro as desired.
13. Serve hot with potato rolls or burger buns lightly toasted with some ghee on a griddle.

Coconut Curry Sea Bass

Prep Time: 3 minutes

Cook Time: 10 minutes

Serving: 3

INGREDIENTS:

- 1 lb sea bass cut into 1-inch cubes
- 1/4 cup chopped fresh cilantro
- 3 lime wedges

For coconut milk mixture:

- 14.5 ounce can coconut milk
- Juice of 1 lime
- 1 tbsp red curry paste
- 1 tsp fish sauce
- 1 tsp coconut aminos
- 1 tsp raw honey
- 2 tsp Sriracha
- 2 cloves garlic, minced
- 1 tsp ground turmeric
- 1 tsp ground ginger
- 1/2 tsp sea salt
- 1/2 tsp white pepper

INSTRUCTIONS:

1. In a large bowl, whisk together all the ingredients for coconut milk mixture.
2. Place sea bass in the bottom of Instant Pot. Pour the coconut milk mixture over the fish.
3. Close the lid and set the steam release handle to 'Sealing'.
4. Select manual mode on Instant pot and cook for 3 minutes.

5. When cooking is complete, press Cancel and use quick release method by turning the valve on the lid from sealing to venting.
6. When float valve drops, unlock lid.
7. Transfer fish and broth into three bowls.
8. Garnish each with equal amounts of chopped cilantro and a lime edge as desired.
9. Serve and enjoy!

Kedgeree - Rice, Salmon and Hard-Boiled Eggs

Prep Time: 30 minutes

Cook Time: 15 minutes

Serving: 2

INGREDIENTS:

- 2 salmon fillets, about 1-1.5 inches thick
- 1 lime zest and juice
- 1 tbsp oil/ ghee
- 1 tbsp butter
- 1 small onion, finely diced
- 1 cup white basmati rice
- 1.25 cups water
- 3 large fridge cold eggs
- 1-2 tbsp fish sauce

Spices:

- 1 tsp turmeric
- 1 tsp ground cumin
- 1 tsp ground coriander
- 1-2 tbsp chopped coriander

INSTRUCTIONS:

1. Measure your rice into a bowl and cover with cold water. Allow to soak for 15-30 minutes and drain well before using.
2. When ready to cook, pop the kettle on to boil.
3. Sit the salmon fillets on a piece of foil leaving about 1 cm between them to ensure thorough cooking and grate over about 1/2 tsp of lime zest and squeeze over half the lime juice.
4. Seal up the foil package and pop to the side for now.

5. Put the Instant Pot into Sauté mode and heat the oil and butter.
6. When hot, add the onion and cook until translucent.
7. Add the spices. Stir well.
8. Add in the rice. Cook for a couple of minutes until well slicked with oil.
9. Pour in 1.25 cups water from the kettle. Stir well.
10. Carefully nestle the trivet into the rice. Place the salmon on one half and the eggs on the other.
11. Press CANCEL and close the pressure cooker lid with vent in sealing position.
12. Select manual mode on Instant pot and cook on high pressure for 5 minutes.
13. When the instant pot beeps, let the pressure release naturally for a few minutes.
14. Using oven-gloved hands, retrieve the eggs and run under cold water to cool them enough to allow peeling.
15. Slice in half. Remove the salmon and gently flake it into 1-inch sized chunks.
16. Add any juice from the salmon to the rice along with 1-2 tbsp of fish sauce to taste.
17. Sprinkle with coriander as desired.
18. Serve by dividing the rice between two bowls and sharing out the salmon and finishing with 1.5 eggs each. Enjoy!

62

Vegan

Spinach Chana Masala

Prep Time: 15 minutes

Cook Time: 25 minutes

Serving: 8

INGREDIENTS:

- 1 cup raw chickpeas
- 3 tablespoon cooking oil
- 1 cup chopped onions
- 1 bay leaf
- 1 tablespoon grated garlic
- ½ tablespoon grated ginger
- 1.5 cups water
- 2 cups fresh tomato puree

For spices:

- 1 green chilly finely chopped
- ½ teaspoon turmeric
- 1 teaspoon coriander powder
- 2 teaspoon chili powder
- 1 tablespoon cholay / chana masala

For finale:

- 2 cups chopped baby spinach
- Salt
- chopped fresh cilantro
- Lemon

INSTRUCTIONS:

1. Wash chickpeas in a cold running water for 30 seconds.
2. Soak chickpeas in 2 cups water overnight. Drain it the next day.
3. Put the instant pot on sauté mode. Wait till it is hot and add in 3 tablespoon cooking oil.
4. Add onions and cook until translucent.
5. Add bay leaf, green chili, ginger, garlic paste and cook for 20 seconds.
6. Add the spice ingredients. Add 1 tablespoon water to avoid masala to burn.
7. Sautee the mixture for 10 seconds.
8. Add the tomato puree, drained chickpeas and 1.5 cups of water. Mix well.
9. Close the lid. Select manual mode on Instant pot and cook it for 15 minutes on High pressure.
10. Let the pressure release naturally and let it cool off for 15 minutes.
11. Vent any steam off after 15 minutes and open the lid.
12. Stir and check how thoroughly cooked the chickpeas are. They should smash up easily without any resistance before putting the instant pot on sauté mode again.
13. Add in chopped spinach and salt.
14. Mash few chickpeas with back of the spoon for thicker gravy.
15. Cook on sauté mode for 3 minutes.
16. Switch off the instant pot. Let it cool down so the gravy will thicken.
17. Garnish with chopped coriander and some lemon juice if desired.
18. Serve warm as a soup. Enjoy!

Black Eyed Pea Curry with Cauliflower

Prep Time: 15 minutes

Cook Time: 30 minutes

Serving: 4

INGREDIENTS:

- ¾ cup black eyed peas
- 1 tsp oil
- ½ chopped onion
- 5 cloves of chopped garlic
- ½ inch ginger, finely chopped
- 2 tbsp. shredded coconut
- 2 juicy tomatoes pureed or 1¼ cup
- 1.5 cups or more cauliflower florets and cubed potato or sweet potato as veggies
- ¾ tsp or more salt
- 2 cups water
- lemon for garnish

For spices:

- ½ tsp garam masala or 1 tsp sambhar masala
- ½ tsp ground coriander
- 1 tsp turmeric
- ¼ to ½ tsp cayenne

Tempering:

- 1 tsp oil
- ½ tsp cumin seeds
- 10 curry leaves

INSTRUCTIONS:

1. Soak the black-eyed peas for at least half an hour in warm water. Drain and set aside.
2. Put the instant pot on sauté mode. Wait till it is hot and add in 3 tablespoon cooking oil. Spread using the spatula.
3. Add onion, garlic, ginger and cook for 5 minutes.
4. Add the spice ingredients and coconut. Mix and cook for a minute.
5. Add pureed tomato. Mix and make it boil.
6. Add the veggies and mix.
7. Add drained black-eyed peas, 2 cups of water and salt. Mix in.
8. Close the lid. Select manual mode on Instant pot and cook it for 15 minutes.
9. Let the pressure release naturally for a few minutes.
10. Open the lid, add lemon.
11. To make the tempering, first, heat oil in a small skillet.
12. When it's hot already, add cumin seeds and wait till they change color.
13. Add curry leaves carefully.
14. Remove from heat.
15. Add the tempering over the curry.
16. Serve as a soup in a bowl. Enjoy!

NOTE:

You can use ½ tsp cumin + ½ tsp coriander instead of ½ tsp garam masala or 1 tsp sambhar masala. Use less turmeric if you are sensitive to the flavor. shredded coconut can be dried or fresh.

Curried Chickpea Stuffed Acorn Squash

Prep Time: 25 minutes

Cook Time: 30 minutes

Serving: 2

INGREDIENTS:

- 3/4 cup dry chickpeas about 1 3/4 cup when soaked
- 1/4 cup brown rice washed and soaked for half an hour
- 2 cups water
- 1 small acorn squash halved (seeds removed)
- 1 tsp oil
- 1/2 tsp cumin seeds
- 1/2 cup chopped red onion
- 4 cloves of garlic finely chopped
- 1/2 inch ginger minced
- 1 green chili minced
- 1/4 tsp turmeric
- 1/2 tsp garam masala
- 1/2 tsp dry mango powder amchur or use 1/2 tsp more lime juice
- 2 small tomatoes chopped
- 1/2 tsp lime juice
- 1 cup loosely packed chopped greens like rainbow chard or spinach
- 1/2 tsp or more salt
- 1/4 to 1/2 tsp cayenne
- cilantro paprika and black pepper for garnish

INSTRUCTIONS:

1. Soak the chickpeas overnight if possible. Soak the brown rice for at least half an hour.

2. Put the instant pot on sauté mode. Wait till it is hot and heat in oil.
3. Add in cumin seeds and cook for a minute or until they get fragrant.
4. Add in onions, garlic, ginger and chili and a pinch of salt. Cook for 5 minutes or until translucent.
5. Add in spices and mix well for a few seconds.
6. Add tomato, lime juice, and greens, cook for about 4-5 minutes or until the tomatoes are saucy.
7. Add in salt, cayenne, chickpeas, rice and 2 cups water. Mix well.
8. Place squash in a steamer basket or steamer plate over the chickpea mixture.
9. Press CANCEL and close the pressure cooker lid with vent in sealing position.
10. Select manual mode on Instant pot and cook it for 15 minutes.
11. Let the pressure release naturally for a few minutes.
12. Open the lid and cancel the pressure cooker mode. Carefully remove the steamer basket.
13. Taste and adjust the chickpea rice stew. Taste and adjust salt and spice. Fill the squash with the chickpea rice mixture.
14. Garnish with cilantro and black pepper as desired. Serve and enjoy!

Vegan Butter Chicken with Soy Curls and Chickpeas

Prep Time: 10 minutes

Cook Time: 35 minutes

Serving: 4

INGREDIENTS:

- 3 large ripe tomatoes or 1 15 oz can diced tomatoes
- 4 cloves of garlic
- 1/2 inch cube of ginger
- 1 hot or mild green chile
- 3/4 cup water
- ½ to 1 tsp garam masala
- ½ tsp paprika or kashmiri chili powder
- ¼ to ½ tsp cayenne
- 3/4 tsp salt
- 1 cup soy curls dry
- 1 cup cooked chickpeas
- Cashew cream made with with ¼ cup soaked cashews blended with ½ cup water
- 1/2 tsp or more garam masala
- 1/2 tsp or more sugar or sweetener
- 1 tsp kasoori methi
- 1/2 moderately hot green chile finely chopped
- 1/2 tsp minced or finely chopped ginger
- 1/4 cup cilantro for garnish

INSTRUCTIONS:

1. Using a blender, puree the tomatoes, garlic, ginger, chile with water until smooth.
2. Add pureed tomato mixture to the Instant pot. Add soy curls, chickpeas, spices and salt.

3. Close the lid. Press Manual and cook for about 10 minutes.
4. When the pressure cooker beeps, press Cancel and do a quick pressure release.
5. Start the pot on saute mode and add in the cashew cream, garam masala, sweetener and fenugreek leaves. Mix well.
6. Bring to a boil, taste and adjust salt, heat, sweet. Add more cayenne and salt if needed. Fold in the chopped green chile, ginger and cilantro. Press Cancel.
7. You can add some vegan butter or oil for additional buttery flavor. Serve hot over rice or with flatbread or Naan. Enjoy!

NOTES:

If you do not want to use nuts, you can use 1/3 cup or more coconut cream instead of cashew cream.

Use all chickpeas, seitan, other meat subs, or veggies to make soy free. When using substitutes that don't absorb much liquid, use larger quantity (for example, 2.5 to 3 cups shredded seitan to substitute the soycurls and chickpeas).

Use dried fenugreek leaves or add a 1/4 tsp ground mustard as substitute for kasoori methi. Use 2 tbsp finely chopped green bell pepper as substitute for green chile.

Mumbai Pav Bhaji

Prep Time: 15 minutes

Cook Time: 20 minutes

Serving: 6

INGREDIENTS:

- 2 tablespoons butter
- 2 onions chopped
- 5 medium tomatoes chopped
- 1 inch Ginger
- 8 cloves garlic
- 3 red chili whole kashmiri
- 1 red bell pepper chopped
- 4 medium potatoes peeled and chopped
- 3 in carrots cutpieces
- 2 cup cauliflower cut in small pieces
- 1 cup green peas
- 3/4 cup Water
- 2 tablespoons Pav Bhaji Masala
- 2 1/2 teaspoons salt or to taste
- 1 tablespoon lemon juice

For Pav:

- 10 Pav or dinner rolls
- 2 tablespoons butter

To garnish:

- 1/2 onion chopped
- cilantro

INSTRUCTIONS:

1. Soak red whole chili in 1/2 cup water for 15 minutes.
2. Grind chili, ginger and garlic along with the water to a paste.
3. Put the instant pot on sauté mode. Wait till it is hot and heat in the butter.
4. Add onions and sauté for 3 minutes. Add bell pepper and sauté for another 2 minutes.
5. Add tomatoes, pav bhaji masala and salt. Add the ground chili paste. Add potatoes, carrots, cauliflower and green peas. Mix well.
6. Press CANCEL and close the pressure cooker lid with vent in sealing position.
7. Select manual mode on Instant pot and cook on high pressure for 8 minutes.
8. When the instant pot beeps, let the pressure release naturally for a few minutes.
9. Open the lid. Use an immersion blender to grind the ingredients.
10. Change to Sauté mode and bring to a boil for a minute.
11. Mix in the lemon juice.
12. Garnish bhaji with cilantro and chopped onions as desired.
13. Slice each pav or dinner rolls in two halves.
14. Heat butter on a pan and place the sliced pav on it. Lightly toast on one side and then turn to toast on the other side.
15. Serve Pav with Bhaji. Enjoy!

NOTES:

The real Mumbai pav bhaji is always made with butter. You can use oil too.

Use Kashmiri chili to enhance the color of the bhaji. You can use another whole chili or red chili/cayenne powder as substitute if you don't have Kashmiri chili.

Bottle Gourd Curry

Prep Time: 10 minutes

Cook Time: 15 minutes

Serving: 3

INGREDIENTS:

- 2 Bottle Gourd or Lauki cut into small pieces
- 1 tbsp Oil
- 1 tsp Cumin seeds or Jeera
- 4 cloves Garlic finely chopped
- 1 inch Ginger finely chopped
- 1 Green chili
- 1 Onion large chopped
- 2 Tomatoes large chopped
- 1 tsp Amchur or Dry Mango powder or 1 tbsp Lemon juice
- Cilantro to garnish

Spices:

- 2 tsp Coriander or Dhania powder
- 1/4 tsp Turmeric or Haldi powder
- 1/2 tsp Garam masala
- 2 tsp Salt

INSTRUCTIONS:

1. Put the instant pot on sauté mode. Wait till it is hot and heat in oil.
2. Add cumin, ginger, garlic and green chilis. Cook until the garlic has turned golden brown.
3. Add the chopped onions and sauté for 2 minutes.
4. Add in the chopped tomatoes, spices and salt.
5. Add the cut Lauki pieces and stir well.

6. Press CANCEL and close the pressure cooker lid with vent in sealing position.
7. Select manual mode on Instant pot and cook on high pressure for 6 minutes.
8. When the instant pot beeps, let the pressure release naturally for 10 minutes.
9. Stir the curry and garnish with cilantro as desired.
10. Serve with roti or rice. Enjoy!

Mushroom Mutter Masala - Mushroom Peas Curry

Prep Time: 15 minutes

Cook Time: 8 minutes

Serving: 3

INGREDIENTS:

- 8 oz Mushroom
- 1 cup Green peas
- 1 tbsp Oil
- 1 tsp Cumin seeds or Jeera
- 1" inch Ginger
- 4 cloves Garlic
- 1 Green chili
- 1 Onion large
- 2 Tomato large
- 2 tsp Salt
- 2 tbsp Coconut cream
- Cilantro to garnish

Spices:

- 1/2 tsp Turmeric or Haldi powder
- 1 tsp Coriander or Dhania powder
- 1/2 tsp Chilli or Mirchi powder

INSTRUCTIONS:

1. Grind onion, ginger, garlic and green chili to make an onion paste.
2. Put the instant pot on sauté mode. Wait till it is hot. Add oil and cumin seeds.

3. When the cumin seeds start to splutter, add the onion paste to the instant pot. Cook for about 4 minutes until the onions turn golden brown.
4. While the onions are cooking, grind tomatoes to a paste.
5. Once the onions are ready, add the tomato paste, spices and salt to the instant pot. Cook for another 3-4 minutes.
6. Add in the green peas and mushroom.
7. Press CANCEL and close the pressure cooker lid with vent in sealing position.
8. Select manual mode on Instant pot and cook on high pressure for 2 minutes.
9. Once the instant pot beeps, quick release the pressure manually.
10. Stir in the cream. Garnish with cilantro as desired.
11. Serve and enjoy!

Vegan Palak Saag Tofu

Prep Time: 20 minutes

Cook Time: 10 minutes

Serving: 3

INGREDIENTS:

- 10 oz Spinach or Palak washed
- 10 oz Tofu Firm
- 1 Onion chopped
- 1 Tomato chopped
- 2 Red Chili Whole (optional)
- 5 cloves Garlic
- 1" inch Ginger
- 1 tbsp Oil
- 2 tbsp Oil for frying Tofu
- Coconut or Cashew Cream to garnish (optional)

Spices:

- 1 tsp Cumin seeds or Jeera
- 1 tsp Coriander or Dhania powder
- 1/2 tsp Cayenne or Red chili powder
- 1/4 tsp Garam masala
- 1 tsp Salt

INSTRUCTIONS:

1. Lightly press the tofu and remove excess water. Cut it in to small cubes.
2. Add 2 tbsp oil in a sauce pan and lightly fry the tofu. Turn the tofu, so it browns evenly. This will take about 5 minutes.
3. Take the tofu out of sauce pan and set aside for later.

4. Put the instant pot on sauté mode. Wait till it is hot and heat 1 tbsp oil and add cumin seeds.
5. When cumin seeds start to splutter, add ginger, garlic, red chili and onions. Sauté for about 3 minutes until onion is lightly browned.
6. Add in the tomato, spices and spinach.
7. Press CANCEL and close the pressure cooker lid with vent in sealing position.
8. Select manual mode on Instant pot and cook on high pressure for 2 minutes.
9. When the instant pot beeps, let the pressure release naturally for a few minutes.
10. Using an immersion blender, blend the spinach and other ingredients in the pot to a creamy texture.
11. Change the setting to sauté mode. Then add the tofu and cook for another minute.
12. Garnish with coconut or cashew cream if desired.
13. Serve with naan, roti or paratha. Enjoy!

Potato & Chickpea Curry

Prep Time: 10 minutes

Cook Time: 20 minutes

Serving: 4

INGREDIENTS:

- 1 tbsp oil
- 1 tsp cumin seeds
- 1 medium red onion
- 2 green chili, sliced
- 3 large garlic cloves, chopped
- 1 inch ginger, chopped
- 3 medium tomatoes, pureed
- 3 white potatoes, diced
- 2 x 15.5 oz can of chickpeas, drained & rinsed
- 1.25 cups water
- 2 tbsp chopped cilantro
- 1/3 cup coconut milk
- 1 tbsp lemon juice

Spices:

- 1.5 tsp curry powder
- 1/2 tsp garam masala
- 1/2 tsp cumin powder
- 1/4 tsp turmeric powder
- 1/4 tsp smoked paprika
- 1.25 tsp salt

INSTRUCTIONS:

1. Put the instant pot on sauté mode. Wait till it is hot and add oil and cumin seeds.

2. Let the cumin seeds sputter and then add chopped onion, ginger, garlic and green chili. Cook for 3 minutes until onions are soft and light brown.
3. Add the tomato puree. Stir and cover the pot with a glass lid. Cook the tomato puree for 5 minutes.
4. Add in the spices and cook for a minute or two.
5. Add diced potatoes, chickpeas and stir to combine.
6. Add water and mix.
7. Add 2 tablespoons chopped cilantro and close the lid. Make sure the valve is sealed.
8. Select manual mode on Instant pot and cook on high pressure for 6 minutes.
9. When the instant pot beeps, let the pressure release naturally for 10 minutes and then do a quick release.
10. Add coconut milk, lemon juice. Adjust spice levels to taste.
11. Garnish with some cilantro and enjoy the curry over rice!

Vegan Spinach Potato Curry - Aloo Saag

Prep Time: 10 minutes

Cook Time: 15 minutes

Serving: 4

INGREDIENTS:

- 1 tbsp avocado oil
- 1/2 tsp cumin seeds
- 3-4 garlic cloves, chopped
- 1 red onion, medium, chopped
- 2 large tomatoes
- 2 green chili
- 1/2 inch ginger
- 6 oz spinach
- 2 medium potatoes, cubed
- 1 tsp coriander powder
- 1/4 tsp turmeric powder
- 1/4 tsp cumin powder
- 1/4 tsp garam masala powder
- water, as needed
- juice of 1 lime
- salt

INSTRUCTIONS:

1. Add the spinach leaves along with little water on a food processor or blender and make a puree. Set aside for later.
2. Next puree tomatoes with ginger and green chili. Set aside.
3. Press saute mode on IP and add oil. Once the oil is hot, add cumin seeds and let it crackle.
4. Add copped garlic, saute till it starts turning golden in color.

5. Then add chopped onions, saute for 2 minutes till it starts changing color.

6. Add the pureed tomatoes, stir, cover the pot slightly and cook for 3 minutes.

7. Remove cover, add salt, coriander powder, garam masala, turmeric powder and cumin powder. Stir, cover and cook for another 2 mins.

8. Add pureed spinach and stir.

9. Cover and cook for 2 more minutes. This is how I covered the IP, don't seal it just keep the cover on top of the pot.

10. Remove cover and add cubed potatoes and stir.

11. At this point add water if you want a more watery curry. I added little water here.

12. Cancel saute mode. Press manual more and select high pressure for 6-8 minutes. 8 minutes will result in overcooked potatoes, if you want your potatoes to be bit firm, go for 6 minutes. Vent should be in sealing position.

13. Once pressure comes off, open the pot and give a stir.

14. Add fresh lemon or lime juice.

15. Serve aloo saag with rice or any bread of your choice. It tastes great with boiled rice.

Hyacinth beans curry - Avarekalu Huli Saaru

Prep Time: 5 minutes

Cook Time: 35 minutes

Serving: 4

INGREDIENTS:

- 340 gms Hyacinth Beans
- 2 tsp Tamarind Paste
- 1 tsp Grated / Powdered Jaggery
- 2 tsp Salt
- 5 to 6 Curry leaves
- 1 tbsp Chopped Cilantro
- 1 tsp Oil
- 1 tsp Mustard seeds
- 2 cups + ½ cup Water

Coconut mix:

- ½ cup Grated Coconut
- 1 tsp + ½ Tsp Cumin Seeds
- 1 Red chili
- 1 tbsp Rasam Powder
- ¼ Tsp Turmeric Powder
- ¼ tsp Hing

INSTRUCTIONS:

1. Rinse the beans and drain.
2. Add the rinsed beans to the Instant Pot and add 2 cups of water.
3. Select manual mode on Instant pot and cook on high pressure for 3 minutes.

4. When the instant pot beeps, let the pressure release naturally for a few minutes.
5. Carefully open the lid and take about ½ cup of cooked beans. Let it cool for 5 minutes. Let the remaining beans be in the Instant Pot.
6. Grind this ½ cup of beans along with coconut mix ingredients into a coarse mix.
7. Set the instant pot in sauté mode. Add the ground coconut mix, jaggery and tamarind paste to the cooked beans. Mix well. If required add more water.
8. Add salt, curry leaves, and cilantro. Let it simmer in sauté mode for 8 to 10 minutes.
9. In a separate pan, heat oil and add mustard seeds and cumin seeds. As they start to splutter add it to the Instant pot and mix well.
10. Serve hot with rice. Enjoy!

Kidney Beans and Spinach Gravy

Prep Time: 3 hours

Cook Time: 40 minutes

Serving: 2

INGREDIENTS:

- 1/2 cup Kidney Beans
- 1 10oz pack Spinach, chopped
- 1 inch Ginger, chopped
- 1/4 tsp + 1 tsp Salt
- 2 cups Water

INSTRUCTIONS:

1. Wash and soak the beans for at least three hours. If you are not able to soak, then increase the cooking time.
2. Add the soaked kidney beans and ¼ tsp of salt to the Instant Pot and add two cups of water.
3. Close the lid. Make sure the valve is sealed.
4. Select manual mode on Instant pot and cook on high pressure for 12 minutes.
5. Let the pressure release regularly.
6. Carefully open the lid and take a ladle full of cooked beans and mash it a bit to thicken the gravy.
7. Set it back to sauté mode and add the chopped ginger, spinach, and the remaining salt. Mix well.
8. Simmer for 7 to 10 minutes or until the spinach is all cooked.
9. Serve and enjoy the gravy!

Channa Madra Gravy - Chickpeas with Yogurt Gravy

Prep Time: 6 hours

Cook Time: 30 minutes

Serving: 3

INGREDIENTS:

- 2 tsp Oil
- 1 Bay leaf
- 1-inch piece Cinnamon
- 4 Cloves
- 2 Green Cardamom
- 1 Black Cardamom
- 1 tsp Cumin Seeds
- 1/2 tsp Hing
- 1 tsp Coriander Powder
- 1/2 tsp Red Chili Powder
- 1/2 tsp Turmeric Powder
- 1 tsp Salt
- 1/2 cup Yogurt
- 1/2 cup Chick Peas
- 1 tsp Rice Flour
- 2 tsp Raisins
- 1.5 cup + 1/4 cup Water

INSTRUCTIONS:

1. Wash and soak the chick peas for at least 6 hours.
2. Put the instant pot on sauté mode. Wait till it is hot and heat in oil.
3. Add cumin seeds, hing, green and black cardamom, cloves, cinnamon and bay leaf. Sauté for a minute and then add the soaked chick peas.

4. Add the dry masalas, turmeric powder, coriander powder, red chili powder, and salt. Mix well.
5. Add 1.5 cups of water and mix again.
6. Close the lid and set the steam release handle to 'Sealing'.
7. Select manual mode on Instant pot and cook on high pressure for 5 minutes.
8. When the instant pot beeps, let the pressure release naturally for a few minutes.
9. Then carefully open the lid and mix it all once.
10. Mix 1 tsp of rice flour in 1/4 cup of water and add this to the gravy. This thickens the gravy.
11. Add 2 tsp of raisins and mix well.
12. Set the Instant Pot to "keep warm" mode and add 1/2 cup of yogurt and keep stirring. Make sure you keep stirring and this prevents the yogurt from thickening.
13. Once the yogurt is completely blended, set it to sauté mode and simmer the gravy for 2 minutes.
14. Serve hot with rice or roti. Enjoy!

Goan Dry Peas Curry

Prep Time: 5 hours

Cook Time: 35 minutes

Serving: 4

INGREDIENTS:

- ½ cup Dried White Peas
- 2 Potatoes, cubed
- 2 tsp Oil
- 2 Garlic cloves, diced
- 1 Onion, chopped
- 1/3 cup Coconut Slices
- ½ tsp Tamarind paste
- ¼ tsp Turmeric Powder
- ½ tsp Sugar
- 1.5 tsp Salt
- ¼ cup + 1.5 cups Water
- Cilantro to garnish

To roast:

- ¼ tsp Peppercorns
- 2 Red Chili
- ¾ tsp Coriander Seeds
- 1 Cardamom
- ½ tsp Fennel Seeds
- ½ in piece Cinnamon
- 2 Cloves

INSTRUCTIONS:

1. Soak the white peas overnight if possible or for at least 5 hours.

2. Put the instant pot on sauté mode. Wait till it is hot and heat in oil.
3. Add the onion and garlic and cook until they are translucent.
4. Remove the onion and garlic. Set aside for later.
5. Add the ingredients to be roasted. Dry roast for a minute and then add the coconut slices. Roast along with coconut for one more minute.
6. Remove the mix and allow to cool.
7. Grind the roasted dry ingredients along with sautéed onion, garlic, and turmeric powder and tamarind paste by adding ¼ cup of water.
8. Add this ground paste, soaked white peas, chopped potatoes and 1.5 cups of water to the Instant Pot. Stir the ingredients.
9. Select manual mode on Instant pot and cook on high pressure for 8 minutes.
10. When the instant pot beeps, let the pressure release naturally for a few minutes.
11. Once the pressure is released, carefully open the lid. Mix the ingredients.
12. Garnish with cilantro as desired.
13. Serve hot with roti. Enjoy!

Dals, Soups and Lentils

Dal Makhani

Serving size: 4

Prep time: 12-24 hours

Cook time: 30 minutes

INGREDIENTS:

- 1 cup whole and split lentils
- 2 tablespoons avocado oil
- 1 tablespoon cumin seeds
- 1 large onion, chopped
- 1 bay leaf
- 3 tsp minced garlic
- 1 ½ tsp minced ginger
- 2 chopped tomatoes
- 3 cups water
- 2 tablespoons ghee
- Cilantro, garnish
- 1 tsp garam masala
- 1 tsp salt
- 1 tsp turmeric
- ½ tsp black pepper
- ½ – 1 tsp cayenne

INSTRUCTIONS:

1. Soak the lentils overnight. Drain and rinse.
2. Press the sauté button on the Instant Pot.
3. Add the oil and wait or a minute till it heats up.
4. Add cumin seeds and cook till they start to change color.

5. Add the onion and bay leaf. Stir until the color of onion turns golden.
6. Add the garlic, ginger, garam masala, salt, turmeric, black pepper and cayenne. Stir.
7. Add the tomatoes. Cook until the tomatoes break down.
8. Add the lentils and 3 cups of water. Mix.
9. Simmer on low heat till the dals are soft.
10. Garnish with olive oil or cilantro if desired.
11. Serve. Enjoy!

Spinach Dal

Prep Time: 10 minutes

Cook Time: 15 minutes

Serving: 3

INGREDIENTS:

- ¼ cup split pigeon peas lentil
- ¼ cup red lentil
- 1 tablespoon vegetable oil
- 3 chopped garlic cloves
- 1 chopped green chili
- ½ teaspoon cumin seeds
- ¼ teaspoon mustard seeds
- 1 large tomato, chopped
- 5 oz spinach, chopped
- ¼ teaspoon turmeric powder
- 1.5 cups water
- ¼ teaspoon garam masala
- juice of ½ lemon
- salt
- cilantro

INSTRUCTIONS:

1. Wash and rinse the dals. Set it aside.
2. Put the instant pot on sauté mode. Wait till it is hot and add in 3 tablespoon cooking oil.
3. add cumin seeds and mustard seeds and let them crackle.
4. Add chopped garlic, green chili. Sauté till the garlic starts turns golden.
5. Add chopped tomato and mix. Cook for a minute.
6. Add chopped spinach and mix.
7. Add salt and turmeric powder.

8. Cook the mixture for 2 minutes.
9. Now add the rinsed dal and stir.
10. Add water and mix.
11. Close the lid. Select manual mode on Instant pot and cook on high pressure for 10 minutes.
12. After 10 minutes, wait 7 minutes more to let it cool down and then release the pressure.
13. Add salt and garam masala.
14. Garnish with cilantro and lemon juice as desired.
15. Serve spinach dal hot with boiled rice! Enjoy!

Lentil & Spinach Dal

Prep Time: 10 minutes

Cook Time: 20 minutes

Serving: 6

INGREDIENTS:

- 2 tbsp coconut or olive oil
- 1 large chopped onion
- 3 minced clove garlic
- 1 tsp ground cumin
- 1 tsp ground coriander
- 1 tsp ground turmeric
- 1/4 tsp dried cayenne pepper
- 1.5 cups of red lentils or yellow split peas
- 3 cups water
- 1/2 tsp salt
- 1 large tomato, cut into 6-8 wedges
- 4 cups of spinach

For finale:

- plain yogurt
- fresh cilantro

INSTRUCTIONS:

1. Put the instant pot on sauté mode. Wait till it is hot and add in 2 tablespoons of coconut or olive oil.
2. Add the chopped onions and cook until translucent.
3. Add in the garlic. Cook for another minute until fragrant.
4. Hit the 'Cancel' button and then add the cumin, coriander, turmeric and cayenne. Mix well.

5. Add the lentils, water, salt and tomato wedges and stir the mixture.
6. Close the lid. Make sure the valve is sealed. Select manual mode on Instant pot and cook it for 10 minutes.
7. After 10 minutes, press the 'Cancel' button, and wait for 10 minutes more before opening the valve to release pressure.
8. Remove the tomato skins and discard them.
9. Whisk together the lentils to emulsify.
10. Smashing the tomato wedges against the side of the pot if necessary.
11. Add the spinach.
12. Garnish with cilantro and/or butter if desired, then stir.

NOTE:

You can use a combination of both red lentils and yellow split peas too. You can also add 2 tsp butter to give a richer flavor, but leave it out to keep it Vegan. Serve over brown rice or with naan, topped with plain yogurt and fresh cilantro.

Black Eyed Peas Lentils Butternut Squash Chili

Prep Time: 20 minutes

Cook Time: 12 minutes

Serving: 8

INGREDIENTS:

- ¾ cup Black eyed peas
- ½ cup red lentils
- 2 tablespoon avocado oil
- 2 cups chopped onions
- 5-6 cloves garlic chopped
- 2 teaspoon freshly grated ginger (optional)
- 1 teaspoon turmeric (optional)
- 1 celery stalk chopped roughly
- 1 cup cubed bell peppers
- 2 carrots chopped
- 2 cups cubed butternut squash
- 1 small zucchini chopped
- 2 cups low sodium veg broth or water
- 5-6 fresh tomatoes pureed
- 1 piece chili in adobo from the can
- 2 cups spring greens (optional)
- Fistful of chopped fresh cilantro
- 1 tablespoon dried oregano
- Salt to taste
- Pepper to taste

INSTRUCTIONS:

1 Soak the Black-eyed peas in warm water for at least 20-30 minutes. Set aside for later.
2 Puree the tomatoes along with the chili in adobo and keep aside.

3   Put the instant pot on sauté mode. Wait till it is hot and heat in oil.

4   Add in the onions. Sauté for a minute. Add in the ginger garlic. Sautee for 30 seconds.

5   Add in the veggies, lentils, beans, broth, tomato puree except BUTTERNUT SQUASH & spring GREENS.

6   Add in the spices except SALT because beans take a bit longer to cook if salt is added. Stir well.

7   Top it with Butternut Squash and do not stir so that it doesn't turn mushy and stay intact texture wise.

8   Press CANCEL and close the pressure cooker lid with vent in sealing position. Press MANUAL high pressure for 6 minutes.

9   Let the pressure release naturally for a few minutes.

10 Open the lid. Add salt and stir.

11 Test if the beans are cooked well by smashing one.

12 If adding greens, press SAUTE and add them. Cook for a minute until they are wilted.

13 Test and adjust spices as desired. Serve and enjoy!

NOTES:

If using any other beans like chickpeas or black beans then use already cooked ones before adding it to the chili as it requires to be soaked overnight and has a longer cooking time than black eyed peas. Adding it raw along with the other chili ingredients isn't recommended as the veggies will turn mushy and loose texture.

You may substitute butternut squash with sweet potato or white potato.

You can substitute 2 teaspoons paprika for 1 piece chili in adobo from the can.

If you don't want to use fresh tomato puree, you may substitute it with canned puree or crushed tomato and not tomato paste.

Lentils with Goat

Serving size: 4

Prep time: 2 hours

Cook time: 30 minutes

INGREDIENTS:

- ½ cup split pigeon peas
- ¼ cup red lentils
- ¼ cup split chickpeas
- 2 tablespoons oil
- 1 teaspoon cumin seeds
- 2 onions, thinly sliced
- 1 lb bone-in goat pieces
- 2 Serrano peppers or green chilies
- 3 teaspoons garlic (minced)
- 1 teaspoon ginger (minced)
- 2 tomatoes (diced)
- 4 cups water
- 2 tablespoons chopped cilantro leaves
- 2 tablespoons chopped mint leaves

For Spices:

- 2 teaspoons coriander powder
- 2 teaspoons salt, adjust to taste
- 1 teaspoon garam masala
- 1 teaspoon ground cumin
- 1 teaspoons paprika
- ½ teaspoon turmeric powder
- ¼ teaspoon black pepper
- ¼ teaspoon cayenne

INSTRUCTIONS:

1. Soak the lentils in cold water for 1-2 hours.
2. Drain them. Rinse and set aside for later.
3. Put the instant pot on sauté mode. Add the oil and wait for it to heat up in a minute.
4. Add the cumin seeds. Wait for them to turn brown, add the onion and goat meat. Stir-fry for 6-7 minutes, or until the meat has browned.
5. Add the serrano peppers, garlic, ginger, and all the spices ingredients. Stir well.
6. Add the tomatoes. Cook for 4-5 minutes until the tomatoes break down.
7. Add the drained lentils to the instant pot.
8. Add 4 cups of water and mix well.
9. Close the lid, close the pressure valve.
10. cook for 30 minutes at high pressure.
11. Let the pressure to release naturally.
12. Add chopped mint and cilantro as desired.
13. Serve and enjoy!

Vegan Curried Butternut Squash Soup

Prep Time: 10 minutes

Cook Time: 40 minutes

Serving: 4

INGREDIENTS:

Soup:

- 1 teaspoon extra-virgin olive oil
- 1 large onion, chopped
- 2 cloves garlic, minced
- 1 tablespoon curry powder
- 1 (3 pound) butternut squash, peeled and cut into 1-inch cubes
- 1 1/2 teaspoons fine sea salt
- 3 cups water
- 1/2 cup coconut milk

Optional:

- Hulled pumpkin seeds
- Dried cranberries

INSTRUCTIONS:

1. Put the instant pot on sauté mode. Heat in the olive oil and add in onion. Sauté for about 8 minutes until tender.
2. Add in garlic and curry powder. Sauté for another minute until fragrant.
3. Press Cancel. Add the butternut squash, salt, and water into the pot.
4. Close the lid. Make sure the valve is sealed.
5. Select the "soup" setting at high pressure for 30 minutes.

6. When cooking is complete, press Cancel and use quick release method by turning the valve on the lid from sealing to venting. Make sure that the pressure is totally released before attempting to remove the lid.
7. Using an immersion blender, puree the soup until smooth. If you don't have an immersion blender, transfer the cooked soup to a blender or food processor to blend. If using a blender, be sure to lightly cover the vent in your blender lid with a dish towel, to help the pressure from the steam release without splattering. Return the blended soup to the pot.
8. Stir in the coconut milk.
9. Taste and adjust any seasoning.
10. Top with hulled pumpkin seeds and dried cranberries if desired. Enjoy!

NOTE:

You may substitute coconut cream for coconut milk.

Curried Butternut Squash Apple Soup

Prep Time: 10 minutes

Cook Time: 20 minutes

Serving: 4

INGREDIENTS:

- 1 tbsp olive oil
- 1 small onion, 85 grams
- 2 ½ tsp chopped ginger
- 680 g butternut squash, diced
- 1 large apple, diced
- 1.5 -2 cups water
- 1.5 tbsp maple syrup
- 1 tsp salt
- 1/8 tsp black pepper

Spices:

- 3 tsp curry powder
- 1/2 tsp paprika
- 1/4 tsp ground cinnamon
- 1/4 tsp cayenne
- 1/4 tsp ground cardamom

To add after pressure cooking:

- 3/4 cup coconut milk
- 1/2 teaspoon sriracha

INSTRUCTIONS:

1. Put the instant pot on sauté mode. Wait till it is hot and heat in oil.
2. Add in chopped onion and ginger. Sauté for 2-3 minutes.

3   Add butternut squash and apples. Stir well.

4   Add all the spices and mix well.

5   Add water, maple syrup, salt and black pepper and mix to combine.

6   Press CANCEL and close the pressure cooker lid with vent in sealing position.

7   Select manual mode on Instant pot and cook on high pressure for 8 minutes.

8   Let the pressure release naturally for a few minutes and then do a quick release.

9   Blend the soup using an immersion blender or use a regular blender. Just make sure that the soup cools down a bit before you try to blend it.

10 Add coconut milk and sriracha (optional) and mix.

11 Garnish with cilantro and coconut cream as desired. Serve hot and enjoy!

Shorbat Adas

Prep Time: 5 minutes

Cook Time: 30 minutes

Serving: 5

INGREDIENTS:

- 1/2 cup Red Lentils
- 2 Garlic cloves
- 2 ½ cups Water
- 1/2 cup Chopped Onion
- 1 tsp Grated Pepper
- 1/2 tsp Turmeric
- 1/2 tsp Cumin Powder
- Half Lemon juice about 2 tbsp
- 1 tsp Salt
- 1/4 cup Chopped Cilantro
- Croutons or panko breadcrumbs to garnish

INSTRUCTIONS:

1. Add the washed red lentils, garlic cloves, chopped onion and 1.5 cups of water to the Instant Pot.
2. Mix well and set it to manual mode for 10 minutes.
3. Let the pressure release naturally and then open the lid.
4. Using a wooden ladle or potato masher, mash the dal mix nicely.
5. Add in cilantro, cumin powder, turmeric powder, pepper and salt.
6. Add one more cup of water. Let it simmer in sauté mode for 10 to 12 minutes.
7. When the soup starts to simmer, turn off the Instant Pot and squeeze the half of the lemon juice and mix well.
8. Serve the soup hot topped with croutons or panko breadcrumbs as desired. Enjoy!

NOTES:

You can add parsley instead of cilantro.

Chicken Mulligatawny Soup

Prep Time: 30 minutes

Cook Time: 35 minutes

Serving: 4

INGREDIENTS:

- 2 Tbsp Olive Oil
- 2 Boneless/Skinless Chicken Breasts cut into 2 inch cubes
- 4 Tbsp Butter
- 1 Onion, diced
- 3 Stalks Celery, diced
- 2 Carrots, diced
- 1/2 Green Pepper, diced
- 3 Cloves of Garlic, minced
- 2 tsp Fresh Ginger, grated
- 1/4 cup Flour
- 1 1/2 Tbsp Madras Curry Powder
- 1 tsp Garam Masala
- 1/4 tsp Nutmeg
- 1/4 tsp Cinnamon
- 1/4 tsp Dried Thyme Leaves
- 1/2 tsp Kosher Salt
- 1/4 tsp Black Pepper
- 6 cups Chicken Broth
- 1 15 oz Can of Diced Tomatoes, drained
- 1/2 cup White Rice
- 1 Apple, diced
- 3 Whole Cloves

To Finish:

- 1 cup Heavy Cream (or coconut milk)

INSTRUCTIONS:

1. Put the instant pot on sauté mode. Wait till it is hot and heat in oil.
2. Add the chicken and stir occasionally until the cubes turn white, but are not fully cooked. Remove from the pot to a plate and set aside.
3. Add the butter, onions, celery, carrots, and green pepper. Cook, stirring occasionally, for a few minutes, until the vegetables start to soften.
4. Add in the garlic and ginger. Stir for 1 minute.
5. Add in the curry powder, garam masala, nutmeg, cinnamon, salt, pepper, and thyme. Stir.
6. Add in the flour and stir well to combine until a paste forms.
7. Add the chicken broth. Stir well to incorporate the flour into the broth.
8. Add the reserved chicken, tomatoes, rice, apple, and cloves. Stir.
9. Close the lid and set the steam release handle to 'Sealing'.
10. Cancel the Sauté mode. Press the Manual button and cook for 7 minutes.
11. When the cooking is complete, let the pressure release naturally for about 20 minutes and do a quick pressure release to release the remaining pressure.
12. Stir the soup and add the heavy cream or coconut milk and serve. Enjoy!

Gluten-Free Indian Kadhi Tangy Yogurt Soup

Prep Time: 10 minutes

Cook Time: 10 minutes

Serving: 4

INGREDIENTS:

For Blending:

- 1 cup soy yogurt
- 2 cups water
- 1 teaspoon salt
- 1 teaspoon sugar
- 1/4-1 teaspoon cayenne
- 4 tablespoons chick pea flour

For the Tadka, or flavoring of the ghee:

- 1 tablespoon ghee or coconut oil
- 1 teaspoon black mustard seeds
- 1 teaspoon cumin seeds
- 4 slices minced ginger thin
- 1 teaspoon turmeric
- 1 serrano pepper sliced thin

INSTRUCTIONS:

1. Use a blender to blend together the yogurt, chick pea flour, water, cayenne, sugar and salt. Don't let it get too frothy, just mix until everything is mixed.
2. Put the instant pot on sauté mode. Wait till it is hot and add your ghee or oil.
3. When the ghee or oil is hot, add the cumin and mustard seeds and let them sputter for 10-20 seconds.

4. Add the serrano pepper, ginger and turmeric.
5. Pour in the blended yogurt mixture and seal the Instant Pot.
6. Press SOUP setting and cook for 6 minutes.
7. When it beeps, allow the pressure to release naturally for 10 minutes then release the remaining pressure.
8. Taste and adjust, garnish as desired. Serve and enjoy!

Red Lentil Tortilla Soup
Prep Time: 10 minutes

Cook Time: 30 minutes

Serving: 2

INGREDIENTS:

- 1 tsp oil
- 1/2 cup chopped red onion
- 3 to 4 cloves of garlic minced
- 1 jalapeno minced (optional)
- 1/2 cup chopped green bell pepper
- 1/2 cup chopped red bell pepper
- 1/2 tsp ground cumin
- 1/4 tsp oregano and thyme
- 1/2 tsp smoked paprika
- 1/4 tsp cayenne or chipotle pepper powder or both
- 1/2 tsp garlic powder
- 1/2 cup red lentils, washed and drained
- 2 cups water or broth
- 2 large tomatoes finely chopped
- 1 to 2 tbsp tomato paste
- 1/2 to 1 cup water or broth
- 1/2 tsp or more salt
- Crumbled tortilla chips for garnish

INSTRUCTIONS:

1. Put the instant pot on sauté mode. Heat in the oil. Add in onion, garlic, jalapeno and peppers. Sauté for about 5 minutes.
2. Press Cancel. Add the rest of the ingredients and water.
3. Close the lid and set the steam release handle to 'Sealing'.
4. Select manual mode on Instant pot and cook for 3 minutes. When cooking is done, let the pressure release naturally.
5. Taste and adjust. Add a dash of lime juice, garnish with chips, avocado and cilantro.

6. Serve and enjoy!

Brown Lentil Soup with Broccoli, Fenugreek & Black Pepper

Prep Time: 10 minutes

Cook Time: 40 minutes

Serving: 2

INGREDIENTS:

- 1/2 cup lentils
- 2 cups water
- 1 tsp oil
- 1/2 tsp mustard seeds
- 1/2 medium red onion chopped
- 3 cloves of garlic chopped
- 1 hot green chile like Serrano chopped
- 1/2 tsp coriander powder or seeds
- 1/2 tsp black peppercorns or use 1/2 tsp freshly ground black pepper
- 1/3 tsp fenugreek seeds or powder
- 1/4 or more tsp cayenne
- 1/4 tsp cinnamon
- 1/2 to 1 tsp turmeric
- 1/2 green bell pepper chopped small
- 1 large tomato chopped
- 1/2 tsp or more salt
- 3/4 cup small florets of broccoli
- cilantro and lemon for garnish

INSTRUCTIONS:

1. Wash and soak lentils for 10 minutes. Drain and add to the Instant Pot with water.
2. Close the lid. Select manual mode on Instant pot and cook on high pressure for 11-12 minutes.

3. When it beeps, let the pressure release naturally for a few minutes.

4. Meanwhile, heat oil in a skillet over medium heat. When hot, add mustard seeds and wait for them to start sputtering.

5. Add onion, garlic, chili and cook for about 5 minutes or until translucent. You can do this on another instant pot. Stir occasionally.

6. Use a small blender or mortar and pestle and grind all the spices together.

7. Add to the skillet. Mix and cook for a minute.

8. Add tomatoes and bell pepper and a splash of water and cook for 5 minutes until tomatoes are tender.

9. Add the mixture to the simmering lentils. Add a bit of water on the skillet to pick up any leftover spices and add to the simmering lentils.

10. Add in salt and broccoli and bring to a boil over medium heat. Continue to cook for 2-3 mins.

11. Taste and adjust salt and heat. Add more water if needed or simmer longer for desired consistency. Cover and let sit for another 2 mins before serving.

12. Garnish with cilantro and lemon as desired. Serve as soup or over rice/quinoa. Enjoy!

Spicy Sausage & Lentil Soup

Prep Time: 5 minutes

Cook Time: 20 minutes

Serving: 6

INGREDIENTS:

- 2 andouille sausage
- 1/2 large onion, diced
- 3 medium carrots, chopped
- 1 C chopped mushrooms
- 3 garlic cloves, minced
- 1 C uncooked lentils
- 1/2 tsp ground cumin
- 1 tsp kosher salt
- 1 14.5oz can diced tomatoes
- 3 C chicken broth

INSTRUCTIONS:

1. Put the instant pot on sauté mode. Wait till it is hot and heat in oil.
2. Add in the sausage and cook until it browns. Add in chopped onions, carrots, and mushrooms.
3. Add in the lentils, cumin, diced tomatoes, salt, and broth.
4. Close the lid and set the steam release handle to 'Sealing'.
5. Cook the soup for 20 minutes on high pressure.
6. When cooking is complete, press Cancel and use quick release method by turning the valve on the lid from sealing to venting.
7. Remove the sausage from the pot and slice into 1/2 inch pieces. Return the chopped sausage to the pot.
8. Serve and enjoy!

Curried Carrot Red Lentil Soup

Prep Time: 10 minutes

Cook Time: 25 minutes

Serving: 4

INGREDIENTS:

- 2 teaspoons olive oil
- 1/2 medium onion diced
- 1 tablespoon grated ginger
- 1 tablespoon curry powder
- 2 cups baby carrots or about 4 medium carrots, diced
- 4 cups low-sodium vegetable broth
- 3/4 cup dried red lentils, rinsed well
- 1 teaspoon kosher salt
- 1/4 teaspoon freshly ground black pepper

Optional garnishes:

- Fresh cilantro
- Coconut milk
- Smoked paprika
- Cayenne pepper

INSTRUCTIONS:

1. Put the instant pot on sauté mode. Wait till it is hot and heat in olive oil.
2. When hot, add the onions. Sauté for 5 minutes or until translucent.
3. Add the ginger and curry powder and stir for 30 seconds until aromatic.
4. Add the carrots, broth, lentils, 1 teaspoon salt, and 1/4 teaspoon pepper. Stir well.

5. Press CANCEL and close the pressure cooker lid with vent in sealing position.
6. Select manual mode on Instant pot and cook for 10 minutes.
7. When cooking is complete, press Cancel and use quick release method by turning the valve on the lid from sealing to venting.
8. Once venting is complete, remove the Instant Pot lid. Let cool for a few minutes.
9. Using an immersion blender or a regular blender, puree the mixture.
10. Taste and add additional salt and pepper if desired.
11. Garnish if desired. Serve and enjoy!

Black Eyed Pea Soup

Prep Time: 15 minutes

Cook Time: 35 minutes

Serving: 8

INGREDIENTS:

- 6 slices bacon
- 1 medium yellow onion, diced
- 2 ribs celery, thinly sliced
- 1 large carrot, grated
- 4 cloves garlic, minced
- 1 c. cubed ham
- 2 (32 oz.) boxes low-sodium chicken broth
- 1 tsp. kosher sea salt
- 1/2 tsp. ground black pepper
- 1/2 tsp. garlic powder
- 1/4 tsp. paprika
- pinch cayenne pepper

- 1 lb. (2 1/2 c.) dried black eyed peas
- 1/2 c. wild rice blend
- 1 1/2 c. chopped collard or mustard greens

INSTRUCTIONS:

1. Put the instant pot on sauté mode. Wait till it is hot and add the bacon. Cook until brown then remove and transfer on a paper towel lined plate. Break or chop into bits. Set aside for later.
2. Add the onion, celery, carrot and garlic in the pot. Sauté for 5 minutes.
3. Add the ham, chicken broth, salt, pepper, garlic powder, paprika, cayenne, peas, rice, greens, and bacon bits.
4. Close the lid and set the steam release handle to 'Sealing'.
5. Select manual mode on Instant pot and cook on high pressure for 28 minutes.
6. When cooking is complete, press Cancel and use quick release method by turning the valve on the lid from sealing to venting and allow for the pressure to release manually for about 10 minutes.
7. Remove the lid and stir.
8. Let the soup cool until it reaches desired serving temperature.
9. Garnish as desired. Serve and enjoy!

Spicy Garlic Dal

Prep Time: 15 minutes

Cook Time: 35 minutes

Serving: 2

INGREDIENTS:

- 3/4 cup lentils
- 2 ½ cups water
- 1/2 to 1 tsp salt
- 1/2 tsp turmeric
- 1/2 tsp paprika
- 1/2 tsp cayenne

For the sauce:

- 1/2 small red onion
- 2 large tomatoes
- 5 cloves of garlic
- 1/2 in ginger
- 1 hot green chile
- 1 tsp coriander powder
- 1/4 tsp cumin seeds
- 1/4 tsp fenugreek seeds
- 1/4 tsp nigella seeds
- 1/2 tsp garam masala

INSTRUCTIONS:

1. Wash the lentils and soak for 5 minutes. Drain and set aside for later.
2. Blend the onion, tomato and all the ingredients for the sauce until smooth.

3. Heat the instant pot on sauté mode. Once hot, add the smoothen mixture into the instant pot. Cook for 7 to 8 minutes, or until it thickens a bit. Stir well and add a splash of water if starting to stick.
4. Add the drained lentils to the sauce with water, salt, turmeric, paprika and cayenne.
5. Close the lid and set the steam release handle to 'Sealing'.
6. Select manual mode on Instant pot and cook on high pressure for 7-8 minutes.
7. Let the pressure release naturally.
8. Garnish with cilantro as desired. Serve and enjoy!

Split Chickpea Soup

Prep Time: 1 hour

Cook Time: 45 minutes

Serving: 2

INGREDIENTS:

Dal:

- 1/2 cup chana dal - split chickpeas
- 2 cups water
- 1 large tomato
- 3 cloves of garlic
- 1/2 inch ginger
- 1 tsp ground coriander
- 1/4 tsp turmeric
- 1/4 tsp paprika
- 1/4 to 1/2 tsp cayenne
- 1/3 to 1/2 tsp salt

To temper:

- 1/2 tsp oil
- 1/2 tsp cumin seeds
- a generous pinch of asafetida hing
- 1/2 tsp garam masala
- 1/4 tsp cayenne
- 1/4 cup chopped cilantro

INSTRUCTIONS:

1. Soak the split chickpeas for at least 15 minutes. Drain.
2. Combine with 2 cups of water in the Instant Pot.

3. Blend the tomato and rest of the Dal ingredients until smooth.
4. Add the mixture to the Instant pot. Select manual mode on Instant pot and cook for 8 minutes in the Instant pot.
5. Let the pressure release naturally for a few minutes.
6. Open the lid and press cancel.
7. To make the tempering, heat oil in a small skillet over medium heat.
8. When the oil is hot, add cumin seeds and cook for a minute or until they change color. Add in the asafetida.
9. Add half of this tempering, garam masala, cayenne to the simmering dal and mix in.
10. Taste and adjust salt and spice.
11. Add cilantro as desired. Garnish with the remaining tempering and serve. Enjoy!

Split Pigeon Peas Soup

Prep Time: 20 minutes

Cook Time: 15 minutes

Serving: 4

INGREDIENTS:

- 1 cup split pigeon peas
- 1 tablespoon ginger-garlic paste
- 1 medium tomato, diced
- 1 teaspoon salt
- 1/2 teaspoon turmeric powder
- 1 teaspoon garam masala
- 1 teaspoon coriander powder
- 1 teaspoon cumin powder
- 1/2 teaspoon cayenne powder
- 1/2 teaspoon dry mango powder
- 2 cups water
- 2 tablespoons chopped cilantro

To temper:

- 3 teaspoons olive oil/ghee/butter
- 1 teaspoon black mustard seeds
- 1 pinch asafoetida
- 1 small onion chopped
- 1 green chili (optional)
- 6-8 curry leaves

INSTRUCTIONS:

1. Rinse and soak split pigeon peas in hot water while you prepare tempering.

2. Put the instant pot on sauté mode. Wait till it is hot and add oil, asafoetida and mustard seeds. Wait for them to spit.
3. Add onion, curry leaves and a green chili. Sauté for 30-45 seconds until the onion turns pink.
4. Transfer the tempering mix in a bowl.
5. Add ginger-garlic paste in the pot and sauté for 30 seconds.
6. Add diced tomato and sauté for another 30 seconds.
7. Add salt and all dry spices and sauté for 30 seconds.
8. Add strained lentils, 2 cups water and stir well.
9. Close the lid and set the steam release handle to 'Sealing'.
10. Select manual mode on Instant pot and cook for 4 minutes. If you prefer a mushy texture, set the time to 6-7 minutes.
11. Let the pressure release naturally for a few minutes.
12. Open the lid after the pin drops. Add the tempering and the chopped cilantro and stir.
13. Serve warm and enjoy!

Beet Rice Pulao

Prep Time: 5 minutes

Cook Time: 20 minutes

Serving: 4

INGREDIENTS:

- 1 cup Basmati Rice
- 1 1/4 cup Water
- 1 tbsp Ghee or Oil
- 1/2 tsp Cumin seeds or Jeera
- 1/2 tbsp Ginger paste
- 1/2 tbsp Garlic paste
- 1/2 Onion thinly sliced
- 1 Beet cut into small pieces
- 1/2 cup Green peas
- 1 tbsp Lemon juice

Whole Spices:

- 1" inch Cinnamon or Dal chini
- 1 Bay leaf or Tej Patta
- 1 Star anaise
- 6 Black peppercorns
- 3 Cloves or Laung

Spices:

- 2 tsp Salt
- 1/2 tsp Cayenne or Red chili powder
- 1/2 tsp Garam masala
- 1 tsp Coriander or Dhania powder
- 1/4 tsp Turmeric or Haldi powder

INSTRUCTIONS:

1. Put the instant pot on sauté mode. Wait till it is hot and add ghee, cumin seeds and whole spices. Sauté them for 30 seconds until the cumin seeds change color.
2. Add the sliced onions, ginger, garlic and sauté for 3 minutes.
3. Add the beets, green peas and spices. Mix well.
4. Add the rice and water to the pot. Stir well.
5. Close the lid and set the steam release handle to 'Sealing'.
6. Select manual mode on Instant pot and cook on high pressure for 4 minutes.
7. When the instant pot beeps, let the pressure release naturally for 10 minutes then release the pressure manually.
8. Add the lemon juice and fluff the rice.
9. Serve with homemade yogurt or raita. Enjoy!

NOTES:

Adding whole spices is optional. If you want to reduce spice, skip the cayenne.

For green peas, you can also substitute potatoes, bell peppers, carrots and edmame.

Beetroot Rice

Prep Time: 15 minutes

Cook Time: 6 minutes

Serving: 2

INGREDIENTS:

- 1 cup Basmati Rice
- 1 medium onion sliced
- 1 cup Grated Beetroot
- 1/2 cup Green Peas
- 3 slit Green chilli
- 1 tbsp ginger-garlic paste
- 1 tsp cumin/jeera seeds
- 1 tsp Biryani masala or garam masala
- 1 tsp coriander powder
- Mint leaves - fistful(optional)
- Curry leaves
- 2 tbsp chopped Coriander leaves
- Salt needed
- 2 cups Water
- 1 tbsp Fresh Lemon juice

For the seasoning:

- 2 tbsp Oil
- 1 Bay leaf
- 2 Cloves
- 1 inch piece Cinnamon
- 1 Cardamom

INSTRUCTIONS:

1. Put the instant pot on sauté mode. Wait till it is hot and heat in oil.
2. Add bay leaf, cinnamon sticks, cardamom, cloves, curry leaves, cumin. Sauté for 30 seconds until aromatic.
3. Add green chilis, ginger-garlic paste and sauté for 1-2 minutes,
4. Add sliced onions. Saute and stir for 2-3 minutes until translucent.
5. Add green peas, grated beetroot and cook for another 2 minutes.
6. Add biryani powder, coriander powder and mix well.
7. Add rinsed Basmati Rice, water, salt and give a stir.
8. Press CANCEL and close the pressure cooker lid with vent in sealing position.
9. Select manual mode on Instant pot and cook on high pressure for 6 minutes.
10. When the instant pot beeps, let the pressure release naturally for 10 minutes.
11. Open the lid after the pin drops.
12. Garnish with Cilantro and lime juice as desired.
13. Serve and Enjoy!

NOTES:

If you are soaking rice before, then add 1.5 cups of water for 1 cup of water.

You can also add finely chopped beetroot instead of grated beetroot.

Meghalaya Style Dal with Sesame Seeds
Prep Time: 10 minutes

Cook Time: 40 minutes

Serving: 3

INGREDIENTS:

- ½ cup Brown Masoor Dal
- ½ cup Toor Dal
- 2 cups Water
- 1 tsp Salt
- 1 tsp Ginger Garlic Paste
- 1 tbsp Black Sesame Seeds, heaped
- 1 tsp Oil
- 1 tsp Paprika

INSTRUCTIONS:

1. Wash the dals and soak for 15 minutes.
2. Put the instant pot on sauté mode. Wait till it is hot and add the sesame seeds. Dry roast for two minutes.
3. Once they start to splutter, turn the Instant pot off and remove the sesame from the pot and allow it to cool.
4. Grind it into a coarse powder without adding any water.
5. Put the instant pot on sauté mode and heat in oil.
6. Add the ginger garlic paste and the dals. Sauté for a minute.
7. Add two cups of water and the salt.
8. Press CANCEL and close the pressure cooker lid with vent in sealing position.
9. Cook on MANUAL high pressure for 10 minutes.
10. Let the pressure release naturally for a few minutes.
11. Once the pressure is released, carefully open the lid.
12. Put the instant pot back on sauté mode. Add the powdered sesame seed powder and paprika. Mix and mash the dal.
13. Let it simmer for two to three minutes and turn off the pot.
14. Serve hot with rice. Enjoy!

Dal Bafla

Prep Time: 20 minutes

Cook Time: 1 hour

Serving: 3

INGREDIENTS:

For the Bafla:

- ¾ cup Wheat Flour
- ¼ cup Juwar Flour
- ½ cup + 1tbsp Water for mixing the flour
- 6 cups Water for boiling
- ¼ tsp + ½ tsp Salt
- 1.4 tsp Turmeric Powder
- ½ tsp Cumin
- 1 tbsp Ghee
- ½ tsp Carom seeds

For the Dal:

- ½ cup Toor dal
- ¾ tsp Salt
- ½ tsp Turmeric Powder
- 1.5 cups Water

For Tempering:

- 1 tbsp Ghee
- ½ tsp Red chili Powder
- ½ tsp Mustard Seeds
- 1 tsp Cumin
- ½ tsp Hing

INSTRUCTIONS:

Preparing the Bafla:

1. Add 6 cups of water into the pot. Add in ¼ tsp of salt and ¼ tsp of turmeric powder.
2. Sauté for about 10 minutes until the water boil.
3. While waiting, you can prepare the dough for the bafla.
4. In a mixing bowl, combine the wheat flour, Juwar flour, ½ tsp of salt, ½ tsp of cumin seeds, ½ tsp of carom seeds and ghee.
5. Add water little by little and mix the ingredients to form a nice dough, about ½ cups + 1 tbsp of water.
6. Divide the dough into equal sized balls. Roll them in your palms to make them smoother.
7. Once the water starts to boil, slowly drop these balls into the water and let it cook for about 8 minutes until they float to the surface.
8. Carefully remove those balls and let them dry for at least 10 minutes. Drain the excess water.
9. Rinse the pot after use to be used in preparing the Dal. Meanwhile, preheat the oven to 350 degree F.
10. Put a parchment paper or aluminum foil in a baking tray.
11. Place the bafla in the baking tray and bake for about 30 to 35 minutes until they are crisp and firm. Make sure you turn once in between. It might take 30-35 minutes. While the baking is happening, you can prepare the dal.
12. After baking, allow the bafla to cool before assembling.

Preparing the Dal:

1. Add the washed toor dal together with salt, turmeric powder and 1.5 cups of water to the instant pot.
2. Select manual mode on Instant pot and cook on high pressure for 12 minutes.
3. When the instant pot beeps, let the pressure release naturally for a few minutes.
4. Use fork to mash the dal.

Tempering the Dal and serving:

1. Use a separate tempering pan and heat the ghee.
2. Once the ghee is hot, lower the heat before adding mustard seeds, cumin seeds, hing and red chili powder to prevent the red chili powder from burning. Mix well.
3. Once the mustard seeds start to crackle, remove from heat and add it to the dal. Mix it well.
4. Take the bafla in a serving bowl and crush them.
5. Drizzle some ghee. Add a scoop of dal on top.
6. Garnish it with cilantro and serve hot.

NOTE:

You can prepare the bafla first, and while you are baking it, you can make the dal. If you are using instant pot for both, wait till the baflas are boiled.

Dhaba Style Dal Fry

Prep Time: 15 minutes

Cook Time: 45 minutes

Serving: 4

INGREDIENTS:

- 2 tsp Oil
- 1 tsp Cumin Seeds
- 1 Green Cardamom
- 2 Cloves
- 1-inch piece Cinnamon
- ½ tsp Hing
- ½ medium sized onion, chopped
- 1 Tomato, chopped
- 1 Garlic, chopped
- 1 Ginger, chopped
- 1 Bay leaf
- 1/4 cup Cilantro, chopped
- 1 tsp Sugar
- 1/2 tbsp Kasoori Methi
- 3 cups + 1 cup Water
- 2 tsp optional Milk/cream

Spices:

- 1/4 tsp Turmeric Powder
- 1 tsp Coriander Powder
- 1/2 tsp Red Chili Powder
- 1.5 tsp Salt

Mixed Dals:

- 2 tbsp Red Masoor Dal
- 2 tbsp Brown Masoor Dal

- 2 tbsp Moong Dal
- 2 tbsp Toor Dal
- 2 tbsp Channa dal
- 2 tbsp Green Moong Dal

INSTRUCTIONS:

1. Wash all the dals and soak for 10 minutes.
2. Put the instant pot on sauté mode. Wait till it is hot and heat in oil.
3. Once the oil is hot add the bay leaf, cumin seeds, cloves, cinnamon, and green cardamom. Saute for a minute.
4. Add the green chili, ginger, garlic pieces and hing. Sauté for a minute.
5. Add the chopped onion and all the spices. Mix well.
6. Add the mixed dals. Add 3 cups of water and mix the ingredients.
7. Close the lid. Make sure the valve is sealed.
8. Select manual mode on Instant pot and cook on high pressure for 5 minutes.
9. After 5 minutes, let it sit for 5 minutes and then do a quick pressure release. Flip the steam release handle to 'Venting' to release the remaining steam before attempting to open the lid.
10. Mash the dal nicely with a potato masher.
11. Add one more cup of water. Add sugar, 1/4 cup of chopped cilantro and crushed kasoori methi.
12. Stir all together. Simmer for 5 minutes.
13. Serve and enjoy!

Special Dalma - veggies and split pigeon peas

Prep Time: 15 minutes

Cook Time: 25 minutes

Serving: 4

INGREDIENTS:

- 1/2 cup Toor Dal / Split pigeon peas
- 1/4 cup Chopped Onion
- 1/2 tsp Turmeric powder
- 2 cups Water
- 1 Cherry tomatoes - 5 or one big tomato
- 1 Medium potato
- 1 Brinjal
- 1/2 cup Chopped squash and carrot
- 1/2 tsp Cumin Powder
- 1/4 tsp Red chili powder
- 3 tbsp Grated Coconut
- 1.5 tsp Salt
- 2 tbsp Chopped Cilantro

For Tempering:

- 2 tsp Oil
- 1 tsp Panch Phoron
- 2 Red Chili
- 1/2 tsp Hing

INSTRUCTIONS:

1. Rinse the toor dal and soak for 10 minutes. Set aside for later.
2. Chop all the required vegetables and set aside for later.

3. Add toor dal, water, turmeric powder and 1/4 cup of chopped onion to the instant pot.
4. Close the lid. Make sure the valve is sealed.
5. Select manual mode on Instant pot and cook on high pressure for 7 minutes.
6. When the instant pot beeps, let the pressure release naturally for a few minutes.
7. After the pressure is all released, carefully open the Instant Pot lid and then mash the dal nicely.
8. Then add all the chopped vegetables, cumin powder, red chili powder, and salt.
9. Close the lid and select steam mode for 5 minutes.
10. After 5 minutes, turn off the pot and open the lid.
11. Mix the dal again and then set it back to saute mode.
12. Add the grated coconut and chopped cilantro for garnish.
13. Let it simmer for 2 minutes and turn off the pot.
14. In a separate pan, heat the oil.
15. Once the oil is hot, add the hing, panch phoron, and red chili.
16. As they start to splutter, add it to the dal mix and mix it well.
17. Serve hot with rice. Enjoy!

Yellow Cucumber Dal

Prep Time: 15 minutes

Cook Time: 40 minutes

Serving: 4

INGREDIENTS:

- 1 cup Toor Dal
- 4 cups Yellow Cucumber
- 2 Green chili
- 2 tsp Oil
- ½ inch Ginger
- 1 tsp Mustard seeds
- 2 tsp Cumin seeds
- ½ tsp Hing
- 5 to 6Curry leaves
- 2 tbsp Chopped Cilantro
- ½ tsp Turmeric powder
- 1 tsp Red chili powder
- 2 tsp Salt
- ½ medium sized onion
- 1 Tomato
- 1/2 tsp Tamarind paste
- 2 cups + 1 cup Water

INSTRUCTIONS:

1. Wash the toor dal and soak it until you chop the veggies. Drain the water and set aside for later.
2. Wash and chop the onion, tomatoes, cilantro and the peeled yellow cucumber into small pieces. Slit the green chili into two. If using ginger, cut them into small pieces.
3. Mix 1/2 tsp of tamarind paste in 1 cup of water and set aside.

4. Put the instant pot on sauté mode. Wait till it is hot and heat in oil.
5. Once the oil is hot, add the mustard seeds, cumin seeds, and hing.
6. As the mustard seeds start to crackle, add the curry leaves and chopped ginger.
7. Saute for a minute and then add the onion. Cook until the onions turn translucent.
8. Add chopped tomatoes and yellow cucumber. Mix well.
9. Add the toor dal, turmeric powder, salt, red chili powder. Mix well.
10. Add in tamarind water, plus two more cups of water. Stir all the ingredients.
11. Select manual mode on Instant pot and cook on high pressure for 12 minutes.
12. When the instant pot beeps, let the pressure release naturally for a few minutes. Once the pressure is dropped carefully open the lid.
13. Set it back to sauté mode and add the chopped cilantro as garnish.
14. Adjust the salt and spices as per your preference.
15. Let it simmer for two more minutes.
16. Serve hot with rice and any curry. Enjoy!

NOTES:

If you don't want the cucumber mushy, cook the dal separately either in the pressure cooker or instant pot. Once the onion turns translucent, you can add the cucumber along with tamarind water, and salt. Let it cook until the cucumber is tender. Then add the cooked dal and other spices.

If using instant pot, after adding cucumber either you can use steam mode or manual mode with quick pressure release for cooking the cucumber.

You can add two to three cloves of garlic. Ginger is optional.

Horsegram Kale Stew

Prep Time: 8 hours

Cook Time: 30 minutes

Serving: 5

INGREDIENTS:

- 3 cups Kale, chopped
- 4 1/3 cup Green Onions, chopped
- 3 Tomatoes, chopped
- ½ cup Horse gram
- 1 Garlic
- 1 tsp Oil
- 1 tsp Cumin Seeds
- ¼ cup Cilantro
- 4 cups Water
- 1.5 tsp Salt

Spices:

- 1.5 tsp Coriander powder
- ¾ tsp Red Chili powder
- 4 tsp Turmeric powder

INSTRUCTIONS:

1. Soak the horse gram dal for at least 8 hours.
2. Drain the water and grind it along with one garlic clove into a coarse paste by adding ½ cup water.
3. Put the instant pot on sauté mode. Wait till it is hot and heat in oil.
4. When the oil is hot, add the cumin seeds.
5. As it starts to splutter, add the tomatoes and cook for a minute.

6. Then add the chopped kale, green onions, spices and salt. Mix well.
7. cover the lid and cook for 5 minutes in steam mode.
8. Once the kale has shrunken, add the ground horse gram dal paste and 2 cups of water. Mix well.
9. Let it simmer for 5 minutes. Make sure you stir the dal for every one minute to avoid the dal browning up.
10. After 3 to 4 minutes, add the remaining water and cilantro.
11. Bring it to one boil and turn of the heat.
12. Serve hot with rice. Enjoy!

Black Chickpeas Stew

Prep Time: 2 hours

Cook Time: 30 minutes

Serving: 4

INGREDIENTS:

- ½ cup Black Chickpeas
- 2 tsp Oil
- 1 Bay Leaf
- 1 tsp Cumin seeds
- ½ cup Onion, chopped
- 10 Cherry Tomatoes, chopped
- 1 tsp Garam masala
- 1 tsp Ginger Garlic Paste
- ¾ tsp Red chili Powder
- 1 tsp Salt
- 2.5 cups Water
- Cilantro to garnish

INSTRUCTIONS:

1. Wash and soak black chickpeas for at least 6 hours.
2. Put the instant pot on sauté mode. Wait till it is hot and heat in oil.
3. Once the oil is hot, add the bay leaf and cumin seeds.
4. As the cumin seeds start to crackle, add the onion and ginger garlic paste. Cook until the onion turns translucent.
5. Add the chopped tomatoes, red chili powder, and garam masala. Mix well.
6. Add the soaked chick peas and salt. Then add the water and stir the mix.

7. Select manual mode on Instant pot and cook on high pressure for 10 minutes.
8. When the instant pot beeps, let the pressure release naturally for a few minutes.
9. Once the pressure is dropped, open the lid and add the chopped cilantro as garnish.
10. Serve it with warm with roti or puri. Enjoy!

Dal with Jackfruit and Blackgram

Prep Time: 15 minutes

Cook Time: 35 minutes

Serving: 4

INGREDIENTS:

- 1 cup Raw Papaya, chopped
- 2 pcs Jack fruit, chopped
- ½ cup Black gram
- ½ of medium sized Onion, chopped
- 2 tsp Oil
- 2 tsp Ginger Garlic Paste
- 2 Bay leaf
- 2 dried Red Chili, chopped
- ½ tsp Panch Phoron
- ½ tsp Cumin Powder
- ½ tsp Coriander Powder
- ¾ tsp Garam Masala
- ½ tsp Turmeric Powder
- 2 cups Water
- 2 tsp Salt
- 2 tbsp Cilantro

INSTRUCTIONS:

1. Wash the dal and soak till you chop the veggies.
2. Put the instant pot on sauté mode. Wait till it is hot and add the oil, panch phoron, dried red chilis and bay leaf.
3. Sauté for a minute and then add the chopped onion. Cook for two minutes.
4. Add ginger garlic paste and cook for two more minutes.

5. Add the chopped papaya, coriander powder, cumin powder, turmeric powder. Mix well.
6. Add the washed dal, jackfruit pieces, salt, and water. Mix them all
7. Select manual mode on Instant pot and cook on high pressure for 10 minutes.
8. When the instant pot beeps, let the pressure release naturally for a few minutes.
9. Let the pressure release naturally and then add carefully open the lid.
10. Set the Instant pot back to sauté mode and mash all the ingredients.
11. Add the garam masala and chopped cilantro as desired.
12. Adjust the salt and spices as per your preference.
13. Let it simmer for 5 minutes.
14. Serve hot with roti. Enjoy!

Salads

Potato Salad

Prep Time:

Cook Time:

Serving: 6

INGREDIENTS:

- 2 pounds potatoes, (bite-sized)
- 2 cups water
- 1 cup diced carrots
- 1 cup green peas
- 1 can chickpeas drained and rinsed (15.5 ounce)
- 2 tablespoons olive oil

For spice:

- 1 1/2 teaspoons cumin seeds
- 1 teaspoon coriander seeds
- 1/2 teaspoon mustard seeds
- 1 1/2 teaspoons garam masala
- 1 teaspoon minced garlic

For Cilantro-Mint Chutney:

- 1/2 cup mint leaves (packed)
- 1/2 cup fresh cilantro (packed)
- 1/2-inch ginger (diced)
- 1/4 cup water
- 2 teaspoons lime juice
- 1/2 teaspoon salt

INSTRUCTIONS:

1. Place the potatoes, water, and carrots into your Instant Pot. Set it to cook on manual mode at high pressure for 10 minutes.
2. Manually release the pressure and remove the lid.
3. Add the peas and chickpeas. Put the lid back and set it to cook on manual at low pressure for zero minutes.
4. Release the pressure manually.
5. Pour everything into a colander. Rinse it with cold water to stop the cooking. Set it aside.
6. Heat the oil in a sauté pan over medium heat. When it's hot already, add the cumin seeds, coriander seeds, and mustard seeds.
7. Sauté for about 2 minutes.
8. Lower the heat. Add the garam masala and the minced garlic. Sauté for a minute.
9. Remove from heat and let it cool down.
10. Add all the cilantro-mint chutney ingredients to a blender or food processor and pulse them until smooth.
11. In a mixing bowl add the vegetables, the sautéed oil spice mixture, and the chutney, and cooked chickpeas. Mix well.
12. Serve hot or let it cool down. Enjoy!

144

Beetroot Salad with Greek Yogurt

Prep Time: 20 minutes

Cook Time: 5 minutes

Serving: 4

INGREDIENTS:

- 2 beets, tops cut off and halved
- 1 cup water

Other Ingredients:

- 1/4 cup cilantro, chopped
- 1/4 cup roasted peanuts, chopped
- 1-2 teaspoons salt
- 1/4-1/2 cup Greek yogurt

Tempering Ingredients:

- 1-2 tablespoons peanut oil
- 1/4 teaspoon mustard seeds
- 1/4 teaspoon cumin seeds
- 1/2 teaspoon turmeric
- salt, to taste

INSTRUCTIONS:

1. Place 1 cup of water into your Instant Pot. Cut the beets in half and place on a steamer basket or on a trivet.
2. Cook them for 12 minutes, using NPR (Natural Pressure Release).
3. Allow the cooked beets to cool before trying to peel, but once they're cool the peel will just slide off.
4. Dice them into even pieces, and combined all the other ingredients except the items for tempering.

5. Heat up the oil and when it starts to shimmer, put in the cumin and mustard. If you don't have mustard seeds, that's fine just double up on the cumin seeds.
6. Once they the seeds start to sputter, turn off the heat and put in the turmeric, allowing it to cook and flavor the oil.
7. Carefully pour this over your chopped ingredients, and mix it together.
8. Chill and serve.

Chana Salad Chickpea Salad

Prep Time: 10 minutes

Cook Time: 40 minutes

Serving: 6

INGREDIENTS:

- 1 cup chick peas
- 3 bay leaves
- 3 cups water
- 1 cup red onion, chopped
- 1/2 cup tomato diced
- 1/2 cup cilantro, chopped
- 1 teaspoon salt
- 1/2 teaspoon cayenne pepper adjust to taste
- 1/4 cup lemon juice

Optional:

- 1/2 teaspoon chaat masala
- 1/2 teaspoon amchoor (dried mango powder)
- 1/4 teaspoon kala namaak

INSTRUCTIONS:

1. Wash and soak chick peas in hot water for an hour. Drain.
2. Put the chana in your Instant Pot along with 3 cups of water.
3. Add the bay leaves.
4. Cook at high pressure for 20 minutes on the BEAN setting.
5. When the instant pot beeps, let the pressure release naturally for 10 minutes and then release all remaining pressure.
6. Mix chopped vegetables, drained chickpeas and all other ingredients. Mix well.
7. Adjust the salt and spices as per your preference.
8. Serve as a side salad or as a main dish for a vegan meal. Enjoy!

Printed in Poland
by Amazon Fulfillment
Poland Sp. z o.o., Wrocław